QUIZ WHIZ

NATIONAL GEOGRAPHIC KIDS™

QUIZ WHIZ

1,000 SUPER FUN MIND-BENDING TOTALLY AWESOME TRIVIA QUESTIONS

NATIONAL GEOGRAPHIC

WASHINGTON, D.C.

Table of CONTENTS

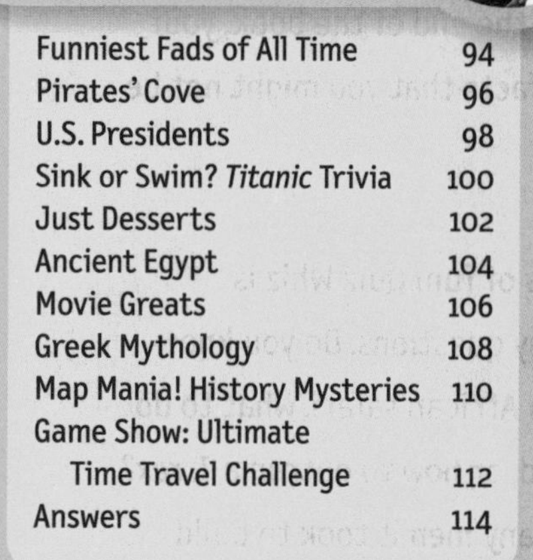

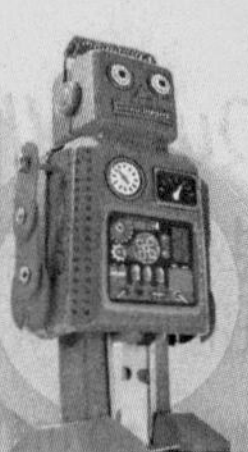

92 Time Machine

134 It's Not Rocket Science

116 Number Cruncher

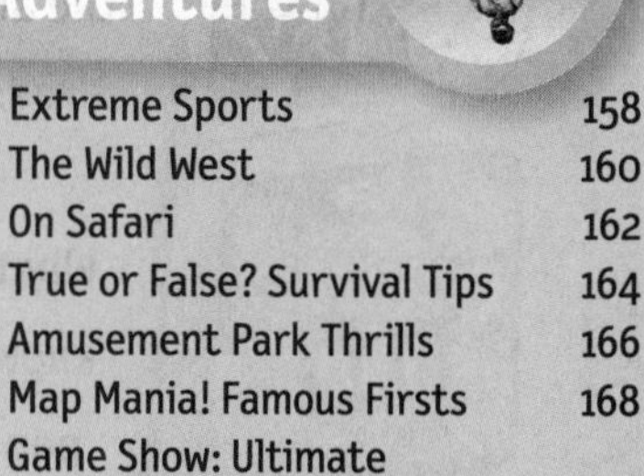

156 Amazing Adventures

174 Credits

INTRODUCTION

Welcome to *Quiz Whiz!* Can you feel your brain getting bigger already? Every time you take a quiz, your brain will start expanding. By the time you reach the end of the book, your head will be bulging with so many cool facts that you might not be able to find a hat big enough to fit you.

Sounds dangerous, but it's actually tons of fun! Quiz Whiz is packed with 1,000 fascinating and funny questions. Do you know what animals you would see on an African safari, what to do if you fall into quicksand, or how to outrun a *T. rex?* Can you guess how many men it took to build the pyramids of Egypt or how long a cockroach can live without its head? Is it really possible to fry an egg on a hot sidewalk? You'll know the answers to these questions—and hundreds more—by the end of this book.

Whether you love animals or spaceships, know everything about rain forests or pop culture, or are expert at video games or *Titanic* trivia, you'll find a place to flex your mental muscle in this fact-filled book.

With many different kinds of quiz games inside, you can pick your favorites or tackle them all. In "True or False?" quizzes, guess if the 30 random statements are fact or fiction. Then flip to the answer pages to discover the many surprising answers. In "Map Mania" quizzes, try to locate animal habitats and famous places—such as the wonders of the world—on the map. Each chapter ends with a "Game Show," where you'll find special photo questions and an extra-challenging "Ultimate Brain Buster." Multiple choice and more true-or-false questions throughout the book cover extreme sports, wild weather, superheroes, sharks, and lots of other topics.

If your quiz *whiz*-dom runs dry, answers to all the questions appear at the end of each chapter. Check your answers for one quiz, or if you finish all of the quizzes in a chapter, tally your score and find out if you hit the jackpot or if your brain is on overload.

Need a break? Quiz your parents and find out if they're really as smart as they say they are! The best part is that it doesn't matter if anyone gets the answers right or wrong. The reward is in the challenge. The whole family will have fun and get even smarter at the same time!

Animal INTELLIGENCE

Animal OLYMPICS

1 **How long can a blue whale stay underwater during a dive?**

a. up to 5 minutes
b. up to 10 minutes
c. up to 20 minutes
d. as long as 3 hours

2 **What was the longest recorded flight of a chicken?**

a. 13 seconds
b. 30 seconds
c. 2 minutes
d. 1 hour

3 **If the following wild cats raced each other, which one would most likely win?**

a. lion
b. cheetah
c. leopard
d. puma

4 **About how many koalas would you have to stack to reach the height of the world's tallest animal—the male giraffe?**

a. 2
b. 5
c. 9
d. 50

CHICKEN

5 **True or False?** The calls of a howler monkey are so loud they can be heard more than three miles (5 km) away.

6 **What kind of animal correctly predicted who would win eight World Cup matches in 2010?**

a. dog
b. pig
c. octopus
d. chimpanzee

HOWLER MONKEY

7. **What is the largest animal that has ever lived?**

a. Komodo dragon
b. African elephant
c. blue whale
d. *Tyrannosaurus rex*

8. **Snow leopards can use their powerful legs to leap how far?**

a. 3 feet (1 m)
b. 6 feet (2 m)
c. 9 feet (3 m)
d. 50 feet (15 m)

9. **Fire ants—stinging insects that live all over the world—can lift more than ten times their body weight! That's equivalent to an average man lifting what?**

a. a chair
b. a refrigerator
c. a small car
d. a jumbo jet

AFRICAN ELEPHANT

10. **An elephant has 40,000 muscles in its ___. That's more than an adult human has in his or her entire body!**

a. leg
b. trunk
c. ear
d. foot

11. **The fastest fish in the ocean can reach speeds of 68 miles (110 km) an hour! What kind of fish is it?**

a. sailfish
b. swordfish
c. great white shark
d. goldfish

12. **True or false?** The world's longest worms can grow to at least 100 feet (30 m) long.

CHECK YOUR ANSWERS ON PAGES 32-33.

DINOSAUR DIG

1 On which continent have the most dinosaur fossils been found?

a. Antarctica
b. North America
c. Africa
d. Asia

2 True or false? Some dinosaurs were the size of turkeys.

3 True or false? Most plant-eating dinosaurs had sharp, jagged teeth.

4 *Stegosaurus* was a plant-eater, but it was no wimp. How did *Stegosaurus* protect itself from enemies?

a. sat on them
b. stomped on them
c. bit them
d. smacked them with its spiky tail

5 If a *Tyrannosaurus rex* were chasing you across a field, how could you outrace this predator?

a. by walking
b. running
c. riding a skateboard
d. zooming away on a motorized scooter

6 Dinosaurs lived at the same time as which of these creatures?

a. early humans
b. woolly mammoths
c. saber-toothed cats
d. none of the above

STEGOSAURUS WITH A FLYING REPTILE CALLED A PTEROSAUR

7 *Brachiosaurus* chowed down on the treetops. About how tall was this necky dino?

a. 11 feet (3.3 m)—about as tall as a Jeep
b. 20 feet (6 m)—about as tall as a two-story building
c. 40 feet (12 m)—taller than two giraffes
d. 500 feet (152 m)—almost as tall as the Washington Monument in Washington, D.C., U.S.A.

8 What is the scientific word for fossilized dinosaur droppings?

a. doodicus
b. streptococcus
c. coprolite
d. giganto stink

9 When the first dinosaur bones were discovered in China 2,000 years ago, people thought they were _____.

a. chicken bones
b. dragon bones
c. tiger bones
d. panda bones

10 True or false? Modern-day birds are descendants of two-legged, meat-eating dinosaurs.

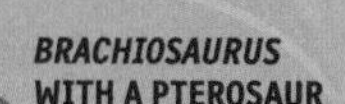

BRACHIOSAURUS WITH A PTEROSAUR

CHECK YOUR ANSWERS ON PAGES 32-33.

SHARK BITES

1 **About how long are a great white shark's teeth?**

a. a half inch
b. 2 inches
c. 10 inches
d. 2 feet

2 **About how many teeth are in a great white's mouth?**

a. 10
b. 100
c. 300
d. 5,000

3 **True or False?**
This shark's skin is so rough it can be used as sandpaper.

4 **Roughly how many shark attacks on humans occur every year worldwide?**

a. 1-10
b. 50-70
c. 220-420
d. 1,500-1,700

5 **Which of these three senses does a shark rely on for hunting?**

a. acute hearing
b. good eyesight
c. strong sense of smell
d. all of the above

6 **How long can a great white shark grow?**

a. as long as a submarine
b. about as long as a jet plane
c. almost as long as a school bus
d. as long as four bicycles in a row

7 **Which internal organ helps a shark float?**

a. heart
b. lungs
c. stomach
d. liver

8 What is a group of sharks called?

a. a shoal
b. a cluster
c. a flotilla
d. a crush

9 True or false? A great white shark can weigh as much as a car.

10 What kind of animal is a great white shark?

a. mammal
b. amphibian
c. reptile
d. fish

11 What is a baby shark called?

a. calf
b. joey
c. pup
d. sharklet

12 What is one of a great white shark's favorite foods?

a. clownfish
b. seal
c. algae
d. tuna steak

13 How fast can a great white's tail propel it through the water?

a. 5 miles an hour (8 kph)
b. 15 miles an hour (24 kph)
c. 40 miles an hour 64 kph)
d. 75 miles an hour (120 kph)

GREAT WHITE SHARK

14 Where did great whites get their name?

a. their big white teeth
b. they are born all white
c. their white eyes
d. their white underbellies

15 Sharks have lived on Earth for approximately how long?

a. 500,000 years
b. 100 million years
c. 350 million years
d. so long that no one knows for sure

CHECK YOUR ANSWERS ON PAGES 32-33.

The Truth About CATS and DOGS

1 **At night, a pet cat can see how many times better than you can?**

a. two
b. six
c. ten
d. twenty

2 **After the death of a pet cat, some ancient Egyptians showed respect by doing what?**

a. shaving off their eyebrows
b. wearing black clothes
c. not talking for ten days
d. lighting candles

3 **Why do cats get stuck in trees?**

a. They like the view.
b. They're afraid of heights.
c. Their claws point the wrong way to climb down.
d. They can't see the way down.

4 **True or false?** Most cats are born with blue eyes.

5 **What is a cat doing when it rubs its body against you?**

a. showing love and affection
b. begging for food
c. cleaning itself
d. marking its territory

6 **Which animals were associated with witches?**

a. black cats
b. white cats
c. spotted dogs
d. pink poodles

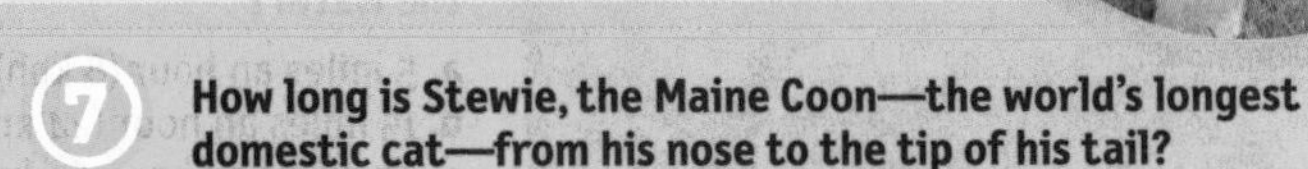

7 **How long is Stewie, the Maine Coon—the world's longest domestic cat—from his nose to the tip of his tail?**

a. one foot (30 cm)—about as long as an iPad
b. two feet (61 cm)—almost as long as two *Quiz Whiz* books lined up end to end.
c. three feet (91 cm)—about as long as a baseball bat
d. more than four feet (122 cm)—that's about as long as a golf club

On *The Simpsons* television show, what's the name of the family dog?

a. Max
b. Bart Jr.
c. Astro
d. Santa's Little Helper

9 **The world's smallest dog breed—the Chihuahua—comes from what country?**

a. Peru
b. Venezuela
c. Mexico
d. Spain

True or false? A dog's nose print is as unique as a human fingerprint.

11 **What job were collies originally bred to do?**

a. sheep herding
b. hunting
c. guarding
d. rescuing

What ancestor do all dog breeds have in common?

a. hyena
b. ape
c. dinosaur
d. wolf

13 **Pugs were favored pets of which rulers?**

a. Egyptian pharaohs
b. Chinese emperors
c. Roman emperors
d. American Presidents

CHIHUAHUA

CHECK YOUR ANSWERS ON PAGES 32-33.

TRUE or FALSE?

Predators and PREY

1. BATS OFTEN GULP DOWN 10,000 INSECTS IN ONE NIGHT.

2. WHEN A SQUID EATS, THE FOOD PASSES THROUGH ITS BRAIN BEFORE REACHING ITS STOMACH.

3. AFTER EATING A SEAL OR SEA LION, A GREAT WHITE SHARK CAN GO FOR A MONTH WITHOUT EATING ANOTHER MEAL.

4. THE BIGGEST SWARMS OF ARMY ANTS ARE MADE UP OF SOME 500,000 OF THESE CARNIVOROUS INSECTS.

5. A THREE-BANDED ARMADILLO RELEASES A FOUL ODOR WHEN ATTACKED.

6. A GRIZZLY BEAR STANDS ON ITS HIND LEGS WHEN IT IS ABOUT TO ATTACK.

7. FLAMINGOS DO *NOT* RELY ON CAMOUFLAGE TO HIDE.

8. THE VENOM OF A BLUE-RINGED OCTOPUS IS SO POISONOUS THAT IT CAN KILL A HUMAN.

9. GIANT PANDAS BARK TO SCARE OFF ENEMIES.

10. A SCORPION SHOOTS WEBS OUT OF ITS TAIL TO TRAP PREY.

11. AUSTRALIA IS HOME TO SEVEN OF THE TOP TEN MOST VENOMOUS SNAKES.

12. A VAMPIRE SQUID PROTECTS ITSELF BY TURNING INSIDE OUT.

13. WHEN A SOARING PEREGRINE FALCON SPOTS FOOD ON THE GROUND, IT CAN DIVE AS FAST AS 1,000 MILES AN HOUR (1,609 KPH) TO SNAG ITS PREY.

14. THE GOLIATH BIRD-EATING TARANTULA GOT ITS NAME BECAUSE IT SOMETIMES EATS YOUNG BIRDS.

15. DOLPHINS HUNT BY CAMOUFLAGING THEMSELVES IN CORAL REEFS AND THEN ATTACKING.

16 THE POLAR BEAR IS A TOP PREDATOR IN ANTARCTICA.

17 A STING RAY CAN STING YOU EVEN AFTER IT DIES.

18 JELLYFISH USE THEIR MOUTHS TO STING THEIR VICTIMS.

19 MEERKATS OFTEN LOOK OUT FOR PREDATORS FROM UP IN THE TREES.

20 WILD HOGS BATHE IN MUD TO CAMOUFLAGE THEMSELVES FROM ATTACKERS.

21 ONE OF THE WAYS A SKUNK TRIES TO SCARE AWAY A PREDATOR IS TO STAMP ITS FEET.

22 CATFISH USE THEIR "WHISKERS" TO FIND FOOD IN DARK, MUDDY WATER.

23 GREAT WHITE SHARK IS ANOTHER NAME FOR A KILLER WHALE.

24 A RED-EYED TREE FROG FLASHES ITS RED EYES TO STARTLE ATTACKERS.

25 A PELICAN ALWAYS KEEPS AN EXTRA FISH IN ITS POUCH IN CASE IT HAS A HARD TIME FINDING FOOD.

26 WHEN PREDATORS ARE NEAR, A PUFFERFISH MAKES ITSELF BLOW UP LIKE A BALLOON BY CHOWING DOWN ON KELP.

27 WALRUSES CAN EAT ABOUT 10,000 SMALL CLAMS IN ONE DAY.

28 JAGUARS HUNT IN PACKS.

29 GOLDEN EAGLES HAVE BEEN KNOWN TO ATTACK DEER.

30 A TRAP-JAW ANT CAN SNAP ITS JAWS SHUT AROUND ITS PREY AT A SPEED OF 140 MILES AN HOUR (225 KPH).

CHECK YOUR ANSWERS ON PAGES 32-33.

Astounding ANIMALS!

BORDER COLLIE

1. **A dog's eye has how many eyelids?**
   a. 1 **c.** 3
   b. 2 **d.** 422

2. **True or false?** Tigers and African lions would meet in the wild.

3. **What is the world's largest rodent?**
   a. chipmunk **c.** capybara
   b. New York City rat **d.** marmot

4. **True or false?** Oceans at the North and South Poles are too cold for animals to live there.

5. **How many species become extinct every day?**
   a. 10 to 20
   b. 30 to 70
   c. 80 to 120
   d. 150 to 200

6. **Where do leatherback sea turtles lay their eggs?**
   a. beaches **c.** ocean trenches
   b. coral reefs **d.** they don't lay eggs

PHILIPPINE TARSIER

7. **True or false?** A lobster has blue blood.

8. **What kind of animal is responsible for the Great Barrier Reef's existence?**
   a. coral
   b. clownfish
   c. conch
   d. shark

9. **What is the most common type of wolf?**
   a. howler wolf
   b. gray wolf
   c. black wolf
   d. jackal wolf

10. **Which of the following is not a type of penguin?**
    a. macaroni
    b. emperor
    c. chinstrap
    d. spaghetti

11. **What is a panda's favorite food?**
    a. wildflowers
    b. snakes
    c. bamboo
    d. peanut butter

12. **True or false?** A crocodile can't stick out its tongue.

13. **What's the name of the dog on the Cracker Jack box?**
    a. Bingo
    b. Snoopy
    c. Max
    d. Scooby Doo

CHECK YOUR ANSWERS ON PAGES 32-33.

MAP MANIA!

GOING WILD!

Help these animals find their way home. Match each animal to the continent where it mainly lives in the wild.

① BOBCAT

② GREEN ANACONDA

③ LEOPARD SEAL

④ TOCO TOUCAN

⑤ ADÉLIE PENGUIN

⑥ IBERIAN LYNX

9 MOUNTAIN GORILLA

10 KANGAROO

11 NILE CROCODILE

12 BENGAL TIGER

CHECK YOUR ANSWERS ON PAGES 32-33.

GO GECKO!

1. A baby gecko is born with a special tooth, which it loses shortly after hatching. What does it use this tooth for?

a. to grind food
b. to kill prey
c. to break open its shell
d. to scratch bites

2. How many different species of geckos are there?

a. less than 50
b. 200
c. 500
d. more than 1,000

3. You can find geckos on every continent except ___.

a. Australia
b. North America
c. Africa
d. Antarctica

4. True or false? Most geckos don't have eyelids.

5. How do most geckos clean their eyes?

a. They blink.
b. They use their tongues.
c. They sweat.
d. They jump in a pond.

6. A gecko has millions of tiny hairs, called setae, on the soles of its feet. What do the setae help the gecko do?

a. climb
b. clean itself
c. fly
d. keep warm

7. Many geckos are nocturnal, which means they are active at which time?

a. in the morning
b. in the afternoon
c. at night
d. all day and all night

8 **Geckos are the only lizards that can do what?**

a. bite
b. eat insects
c. lay eggs
d. vocalize to communicate

9 **As geckos grow, they shed their old skin to make way for new skin. What do they do with the old skin?**

a. throw it away
b. use it as a sleeping bag
c. eat it
d. leave it alone

10 **True or false?**
If a gecko loses its tail it can grow back.

11 **What happens to the tail once it falls off?**

a. It keeps twitching for a few minutes.
b. Nothing, it just lies there.
c. It grows a new body and head.
d. It melts away the first time it rains.

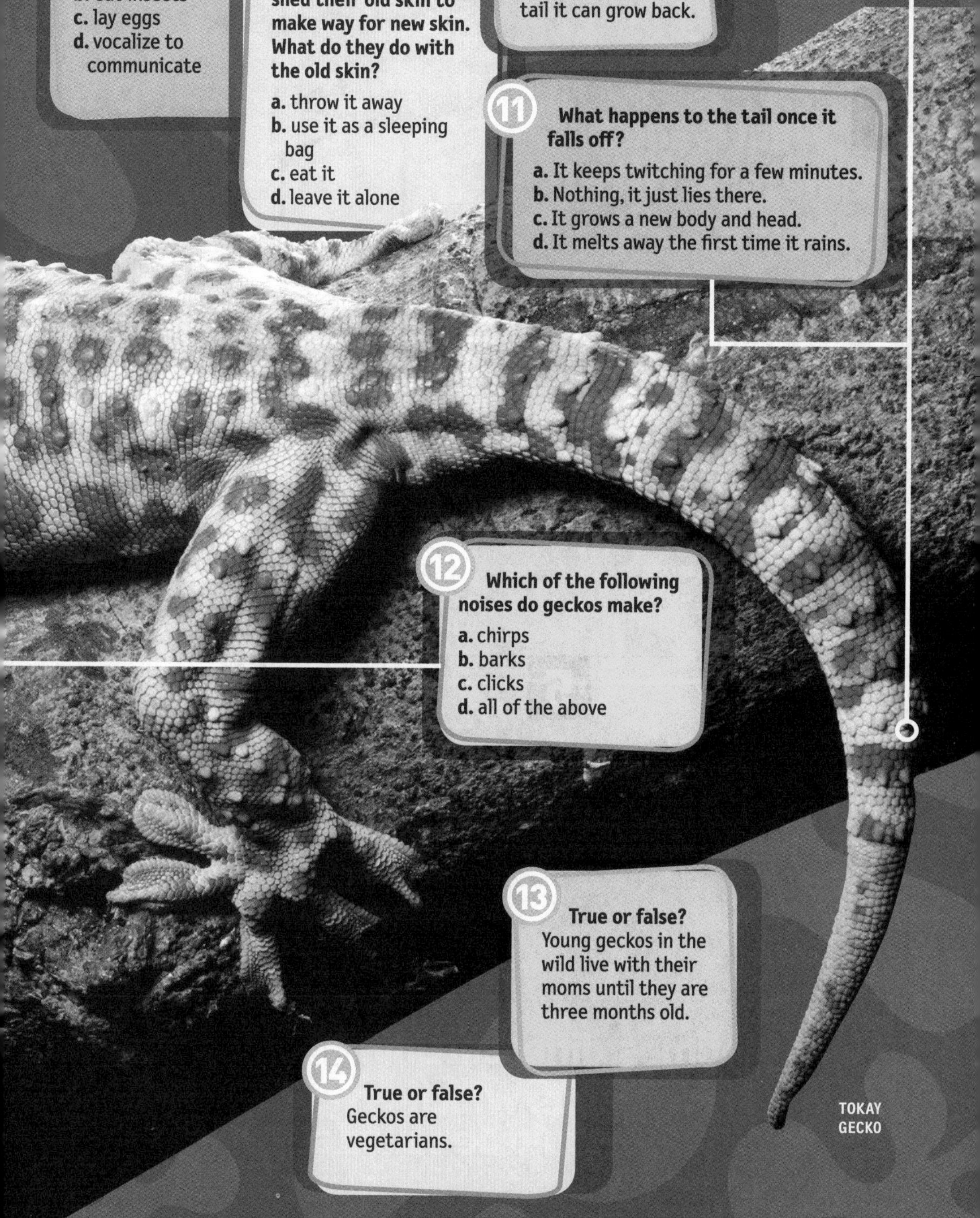

12 **Which of the following noises do geckos make?**

a. chirps
b. barks
c. clicks
d. all of the above

13 **True or false?**
Young geckos in the wild live with their moms until they are three months old.

14 **True or false?**
Geckos are vegetarians.

TOKAY GECKO

CHECK YOUR ANSWERS ON PAGES 32-33.

ANIMAL GROUPIES

1 What is another name for a litter of kittens?

a. crew
b. nest
c. kindle
d. nook

2 Which sea creature would *not* travel in a school?

a. a shark
b. a dolphin
c. an eel
d. a marlin

3 If you saw hundreds of grasshoppers approaching, you'd be correct if you called them a(n) _____.

a. cloud
b. pod
c. army
d. troop

4 A "coterie" refers to a group of _____.

a. peacocks
b. prairie dogs
c. butterflies
d. ducks

5 A _____ is another name for a swarm of locusts.

a. plague
b. school
c. herd
d. mob

6 True or false? A group of crows can be called a murder.

7 Sometimes, different animals have the same group name. Which two of these animal groups would be called an "army"?

a. grasshoppers and elephants
b. caterpillars and frogs
c. grasshoppers and caterpillars
d. caterpillars and elephants

PINK FLAMINGOS

8 **True or false?** Walruses live together in groups called prides.

9 Which of the following words is *not* used to describe **a group of giraffes?**

a. herd
b. corps
c. tower
d. height

10 Which of these is the name for a group of **rhinos?**

a. crash
b. knot
c. gaggle
d. stand

11 Which of the following words can be used to describe a **group of oxen?**

a. team
b. yoke
c. drove
d. all of the above

12 **True or false?** A group of goldfish is called a troubling.

13 As many as **40 meerkats** have been known to live together in groups called ______.

a. mobs
b. herds
c. tribes
d. offices

14 A leatherback turtle may snack on a **smack of** ___.

a. krill
b. plankton
c. jellyfish
d. sharks

15 A **group** of flamingos is called a ______.

a. pink
b. stand
c. leg
d. snooze

CHECK YOUR ANSWERS ON PAGES 32-33.

ANIMAL Speak

1 **When a bee finds food, it alerts other bees to its location by ____.**

a. dancing
b. purring
c. buzzing
d. barking

2 **Cheetahs communicate with lots of noises, but which one of these sounds will you *never* hear a cheetah make?**

a. purr
b. hiss
c. growl
d. roar

3 **What would an ant do to express "Danger ahead!"?**

a. secrete chemicals
b. run toward water
c. roll on its back
d. squeal

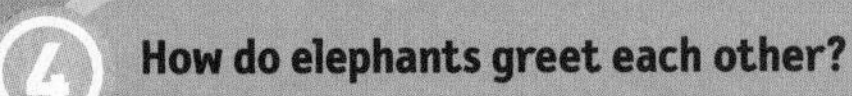

4 **How do elephants greet each other?**

a. swat each other with their tails
b. run around in circles
c. butt heads
d. entwine their trunks

5 **What are some sounds that dolphins use to communicate?**

a. whistles
b. squeaks
c. clicks
d. all of the above

6 **True or false?** Carnivorous fish called piranhas can bark.

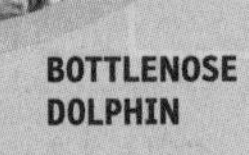

BOTTLENOSE DOLPHIN

PIRANHA

NORTHERN SAW-WHET OWL

7 **Which of the following is *not* a form of wolf communication?**

a. howling
b. scent secretions
c. body language
d. mooing

8 **To attract a mate, owls may ____.**

a. sing
b. sleep
c. dance
d. howl

9 **True or false?** Snakes stick out their tongues to communicate with each other.

10 **A lion's roar can be heard miles away. The roar most likely tells other lions:**

a. "This is *my* piece of land!"
b. "Come over and play!"
c. "I'm so bored."
d. "Let's find an antelope to pick on."

11 **True or false?** Zebras may use their unique stripes to help identify each other.

12 **What does an adult male walrus use the air pouch in its throat for?**

a. as a pillow
b. to sing
c. to call out to female walruses
d. to blow bubbles

PACIFIC WALRUS

CHECK YOUR ANSWERS ON PAGES 32-33.

GAME SHOW

ULTIMATE ANIMAL CHALLENGE

1

Which bird can fly backward?

a. eagle
b. bluebird
c. parrot
d. hummingbird

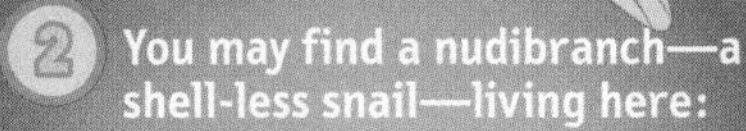

2 **You may find a nudibranch—a shell-less snail—living here:**

a. in a desert burrow
b. on a tree in the rain forest
c. under a rock on the seafloor
d. on an Arctic glacier

3

The heart of a blue whale weighs as much as which of the following animals?

a. dog **c.** zebra
b. wild hog **d.** hippo

4

How many eyes do most spiders have?

a. 2
b. 6
c. 8
d. 12

JUMPING SPIDER

5

A baby kangaroo is as long as a ______.

a. paper clip
b. candy bar
c. pencil
d. ruler

6

The U.S. national bird is the bald eagle, but what did Benjamin Franklin want it to be?

a. hawk **c.** owl
b. dove **d.** turkey

7

A butterfly uses which body part to taste food?

a. antenna
b. wings
c. feet
d. eyes

8 What color is a polar bear's skin?

a. white
b. pink
c. brown
d. black

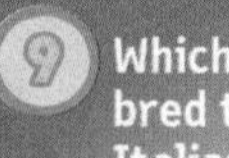

9 Which of these dogs was once bred to be a rescue dog in the Italian and Swiss Alps?

a. 
Chihuahua

b. 
Great Dane

c. 

Shih tzu

d. 
Saint Bernard

10 What is this dung beetle feeding on?

a. dirt
b. animal droppings
c. hay
d. a baseball

11 A baby rabbit is called a ____.

a. kitten
b. doe
c. buck
d. hare

12 Which of these animals would you *not* find in the African savanna?

a. lion
b. antelope
c. gray wolf
d. hyena

13 What color is a hippo's sweat?

a. blue
b. hot pink
c. red
d. green

14 **TRUE OR FALSE?**

Male seahorses give birth to baby seahorses.

CAN YOU IDENTIFY THE BABY ANIMAL IN THIS PICTURE?

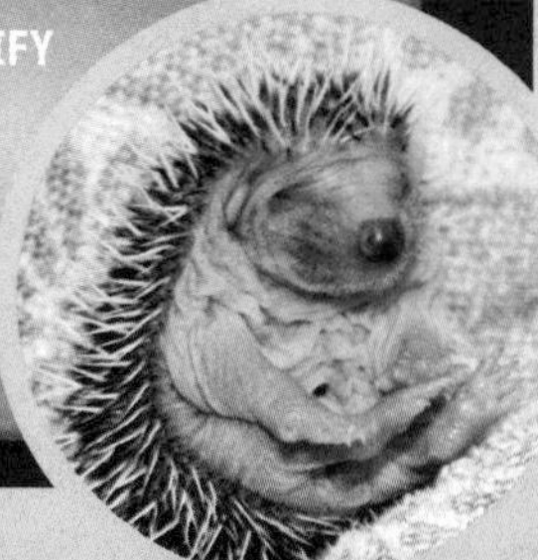

CHECK YOUR ANSWERS ON PAGES 32-33.

ANSWERS

Animal Olympics, pages 10-11

1. **c**
2. **a**
3. **b**
4. **c**
5. **True.** A howler monkey's loud calls tell other monkeys to keep away from its territory.
6. **c**
7. **c**
8. **d**
9. **c**
10. **b**
11. **a**
12. **True.** These superlong creatures, called bootlace worms, are most common along the coasts of Great Britain.

Dinosaur Dig, pages 12-13

1. **b**
2. **True.** Some dinosaur species were small enough to hold in your hand; others were taller than houses.
3. **False.** Plant-eaters had peglike teeth to rake or slice leaves from trees. Meat-eating dinosaurs had sharp teeth to tear into prey.
4. **d**
5. **d**
6. **d**
7. **c**
8. **c**
9. **b**
10. **True.** Birds are descendants of dinosaurs called theropods.

Shark Bites, pages 14-15

1. **b**
2. **c**
3. **True.** The great white shark's skin is made of tiny, toothlike structures that make it feel rough.
4. **b**
5. **d**
6. **c**
7. **d**
8. **a**
9. **True.** Great white sharks can weigh more than 5,000 pounds (2,268 kg).
10. **d**
11. **c**
12. **b**
13. **b**
14. **d**
15. **c**

The Truth About Cats and Dogs, pages 16-17

1. **b**
2. **a**
3. **c**
4. **True.** When kittens are born, they don't have as much of the pigment that darkens their eyes. This changes after a few weeks, when most cats' eyes turn green.
5. **d**
6. **a**
7. **d**
8. **d**
9. **c**
10. **True.** In fact, nose prints have been used to help identify missing dogs.
11. **a**
12. **d**
13. **b**

True or False? Predators and Prey, pages 18-19

1. **False.** A bat can eat some 3,000 insects in one night.
2. **True.** Food must travel through a squid's esophagus, which passes through the brain to get to its stomach.
3. **True.** A shark stores nutrients from food in oil in its liver, allowing the shark to go for a long time without eating.
4. **False.** There can be up to two million army ants in a swarm.
5. **False.** When attacked, a three-banded armadillo will curl up into a ball.
6. **False.** Grizzly bears stand on their hind legs to better see or smell something.
7. **True.** A flamingo's pink color isn't camouflage; it helps the bird attract a mate.
8. **True.** Just one bite from a blue-ringed octopus can kill a human in minutes.
9. **True.** Giant pandas sometimes growl and swat at enemies, too.
10. **False.** A scorpion uses its tail to sting its prey.
11. **True.** This includes the inland taipan, a snake with venom that is 50 times stronger than a cobra's venom.
12. **True.** The vampire squid curls an arm and part of its body up around its head to reveal the darker parts of its body, confusing predators.
13. **False.** It can dive as fast as 200 miles an hour (161 kph).
14. **True.** The goliath bird-eating tarantula, which is about the size of a dinner plate, got its name because it has been known to prey on young birds. More common snacks are insects, frogs, lizards, and rodents.
15. **False.** Dolphins round up schools of fish and then take turns attacking.
16. **False.** The top predator in Antarctica is the leopard seal. Polar bears live only in the Arctic.
17. **True.** If you step on a dead stingray's tail, you can get stung.
18. **False.** Jellyfish have stinging tentacles.
19. **False.** They stand up on their hind legs for a better view from the ground.
20. **False.** Wild hogs bathe in mud to cool themselves.
21. **True.** A skunk has many defense mechanisms, including stamping its feet, pretending to charge, and releasing a stinky spray.
22. **True.** These whiskers, or barbels, are used to touch and taste their surroundings.
23. **False.** Sharks are fish and killer whales are mammals. Orca is another name for a killer whale.
24. **True.** Predators such as birds and snakes may be surprised by the frog's brightly colored eyes.
25. **False.** Pelicans catch fish in their pouches and then swallow immediately.
26. **False.** A pufferfish expands by gulping down water.
27. **True.** A walrus consumes 100 pounds (45 kg) of food every day.
28. **False.** Jaguars hunt alone.
29. **True.** Golden eagles have been known to attack animals as large as deer, mountain goats, and wolves.
30. **True.** The ant uses its jaws to snap up prey, including termites and wood lice.

Astounding Animals! pages 20-21

1. **c**
2. **False.** Wild African lions live in Africa, while tigers live in Asia.
3. **c**
4. **False.** Many animals, such as polar bears in the Arctic and penguins in Antarctica, are adapted to these icy-cold environments.
5. **d**
6. **a**
7. **True.** Lobsters have a copper-rich protein in their blood, called haemocyanin, which makes it look blue.
8. **a**
9. **b**
10. **d**
11. **c**
12. **True.** A crocodile can't stick out its tongue because a membrane holds it in place.
13. **c**

Map Mania! Going Wild! pages 22-23

1. **North America**
2. **South America**
3. **Antarctica**
4. **South America**
5. **Antarctica**
6. **Europe**
7. **Asia**
8. **Australia and Oceania**
9. **Africa**
10. **Australia**
11. **Africa**
12. **Asia**

Go Gecko! pages 24-25

1. **c**
2. **d**

3. **d**
4. **True.** Instead of eyelids, most geckos have a transparent scale that covers and protects their eyes.
5. **b**
6. **a**
7. **c**
8. **d**
9. **c**
10. **True.** Geckos are able to grow their tails back if they lose them to predators. But the new tails are not as strong.
11. **a**
12. **d**
13. **False.** Wild baby geckos are on their own as soon as they are born.
14. **False.** In addition to eating flowers and fruit, geckos also eat insects.

Animal Groupies, pages 26-27

1. **c**
2. **c**
3. **a**
4. **b**
5. **a**
6. **True.** A group of crows can be called a murder or a flock.
7. **b**
8. **False.** Walruses live together in herds or pods. A group of lions is called a pride.
9. **d**
10. **a**
11. **d**
12. **True.** A group of goldfish can be called a troubling, a school, or a glint.
13. **a**
14. **c**
15. **b**

Animal Speak, pages 28-29

1. **a**
2. **d**
3. **a**
4. **d**
5. **d**
6. **True.** Some piranhas make barking, croaking, and clicking noises.
7. **d**
8. **a**
9. **False.** Snakes stick out their tongues to smell. To communicate, they sometimes use body movements and scents.
10. **a**
11. **True.** A zebra's stripes are as unique as a human's fingerprint.
12. **c**

Game Show: Ultimate Animal Challenge, pages 30-31

1. **d**
2. **c**
3. **d**
4. **c**
5. **a**
6. **d**
7. **c**
8. **d**
9. **d**
10. **b**
11. **a**
12. **c**
13. **c**
14. **True.** After a female seahorse deposits eggs into a pouch on the male's stomach, the male fertilizes the eggs and the babies grow inside the pouch.
15. **Hedgehog**

SCORING

0-54

YOU'RE IN THE DOGHOUSE!

You may be in trouble if your pet finds out about this score. But don't worry, you can make him or her proud. Check out your local zoo or aquarium to become an animal expert.

55-108

YOU HAVE ANIMAL INSTINCTS!

You have strong spidey sense and keep your eye on the wild world of animals. Keep looking and discovering.

109-162

YOU ARE THE KING OF THE JUNGLE!

Whether they're four-legged or finned, you love all animals and want to know everything about them. One day you might be a veterinarian or a marine biologist.

AROUND THE WORLD

FIRST STOP, THE QUEEN'S PALACE. NEXT, OUR WORLD TOUR!

BRITISH SOLDIERS MARCH IN A PARADE CELEBRATING THE QUEEN OF ENGLAND'S BIRTHDAY.

I HOPE THIS HAT FITS ON THE PLANE.

HAPPY HOLIDAYS!

1 True or false? The Chinese New Year always takes place on January 1.

2 Which of these trees is most often used as a Christmas tree?

a. fir
b. birch
c. palm
d. weeping willow

3 True or false? Each November, a town in Thailand prepares a special feast for local wild monkeys.

4 About how many turkeys are eaten each year on Thanksgiving?

a. 1 million
b. 5 million
c. 20 million
d. 45 million

5 In what country do people celebrate the Day of the Dead?

a. Ireland
b. Japan
c. Mexico
d. Morocco

6 True or false? A shamrock, worn by many people on St. Patrick's Day, is a four-leaf clover.

7 Which vegetable was used to make Halloween jack-o'-lanterns, before people started using pumpkins?

a. spinach
b. celery
c. carrots
d. turnips

8 According to legend, what happens if a groundhog sees its shadow on Groundhog Day?

a. there will be six more weeks of winter
b. spring has officially begun
c. there will be no summer
d. winter will last all year

9 In 2011, the most popular Halloween costume for pets was a ___.

a. pumpkin
b. hot dog
c. pirate
d. ghost

10 Rio de Janeiro, Brazil, is famous for its celebration of ___, during which thousands of people in costumes parade through the streets.

a. Carnival
b. St. Patrick's Day
c. Christmas
d. Presidents' Day

11 During the Jewish holiday Hanukkah, kids receive gifts of chocolate candies that are shaped like what?

a. menorahs
b. flowers
c. stars
d. coins

12 Which holiday—celebrated from December 26 to January 1—means "first fruits" in the African language called Swahili?

a. Ramadan
b. Christmas
c. Kwanzaa
d. New Year's Day

13 On May Day, children in England welcome spring by dancing around what?

a. a chocolate fountain
b. a piñata
c. a maypole
d. a bean stalk

14 If all of the candy conversation hearts made every year—sold mostly for Valentine's Day—were lined up, how far would they stretch?

a. ten city blocks
b. around the Earth
c. to the moon
d. across the United States twice

CHECK YOUR ANSWERS ON PAGES 54-55.

GRAND CANYON ADVENTURE

1 The Grand Canyon is one of the top tourist destinations in the United States. How many people visit each year?

a. 100,000
b. 500,000
c. 1 million
d. 5 million

2 You can go white-water rafting down which river that flows through the Grand Canyon?

a. Rio Grande
b. Mississippi
c. Colorado
d. Missouri

3 True or false? The bottom layers of rock are the oldest, while the top layers are the youngest.

4 True or false? No one lives in the Grand Canyon.

5 The canyon's red rocks get their color from ___, just like the soil on Mars.

a. iron
b. nickel
c. silver
d. gold

6 Which of the following is *not* one of the ways you can explore the Grand Canyon?

a. on foot
b. raft
c. Jeep
d. mule

7 There are four different wildlife zones in the Grand Canyon. The Canadian Zone is located at an elevation of 9,000 feet (2,743 m). Which of these animals lives in this zone?

a. llamas
b. buffalo
c. wild turkeys
d. pandas

8 Which of these animals does *not* live in the Grand Canyon?

a. koalas
b. peacocks
c. mountain lions
d. a and b

9 Which of these plants grows in the Grand Canyon?

a. palm tree
b. redwood tree
c. cactus
d. cherry blossom

10 Which of these birds would you *not* find in the Grand Canyon?

a. raven
b. hummingbird
c. roadrunner
d. flamingo

11 To what state would you travel to visit the Grand Canyon?

a. Colorado
b. Arizona
c. Wyoming
d. New Mexico

12 How long did it take for the Grand Canyon to form?

a. 10,000 years
b. 100,000 years
c. 2 million years
d. 17 million years

13 True or false? Nearly 40 layers of rock have been identified in the Grand Canyon's walls.

14 If you were standing at the rim of the canyon, how far would you have to hike to get to the bottom?

a. 1 mile (1.6 km)
b. 10 miles (16.1 km)
c. 50 miles (80.5 km)
d. 100 miles (160.9 km)

15 What's the name of the glass-bottomed bridge from which you can peer 4,000 feet (1,219 m) into the depths of the Grand Canyon?

a. Canyon View
b. Skywalk
c. Rock Walk
d. Don't Look Down

CHECK YOUR ANSWERS ON PAGES 54-55.

What's on THE MENU?

1. **True or false?** Scorpions are considered a tasty treat in China.

2. **If you ordered bratwurst in Germany, you'd be asking for what kind of food?**
   a. pretzel
   b. sausage
   c. cake
   d. fruit

3. **You may want to pinch your nose while eating durian, a fruit from Southeast Asia. The smell of durian has been compared to what?**
   a. turpentine
   b. a campground toilet
   c. rotting fish
   d. all of the above

4. **If you walked into a McDonald's in Norway, you'd find a McLacks on the menu. What's a McLacks? (Hint: "Lacks" is pronounced like "lox.")**
   a. a salmon burger
   b. a turkey burger
   c. a veggie burger
   d. a regular hamburger

5. **In the United States, some people eat turducken instead of a traditional turkey for Thanksgiving. What is this dish?**
   a. a vegetarian turkey made of soybeans
   b. tofu lasagna
   c. duck stew
   d. a chicken stuffed into a duck stuffed into a turkey

6. **Which country is the world's leading banana grower?**
   a. United States
   b. India
   c. Denmark
   d. Argentina

7. **True or false?** "Swiss cheese" is always made in Switzerland.

8. **True or false?** Modern-day pizza was inspired by the colors of the Italian flag.

9. **What food was named for the rolled packs that *burros* (the Spanish word for donkeys) often carried on their backs in Mexico?**
   - **a.** enchilada
   - **b.** taco
   - **c.** burrito
   - **d.** nachos

10. **In Jamaica, the word "jerk" is used to describe what?**
    - **a.** a type of candy
    - **b.** spiced and grilled meat
    - **c.** a crop of plantains
    - **d.** a mean person

11. **The deep-fried Mars bar was created in what country?**
    - **a.** United States
    - **b.** Kenya
    - **c.** Scotland
    - **d.** Spain

12. **Which is not the name of an English food?**
    - **a.** bubble and squeak
    - **b.** parson's nose
    - **c.** candyfloss
    - **d.** potter pie

CHECK YOUR ANSWERS ON PAGES 54-55.

The Wide WORLD OF SPORTS

1 **One of the world's most popular sports is known as "soccer" in Australia, Canada, New Zealand, and the U.S. But what is it called in most other countries?**

a. kickball
b. goalkeeper
c. World Cup
d. football

2 **True or false?** Each of the five Olympic rings is a different color to represent the five major regions of the world involved in the Olympics.

3 **What is the name of the sport, popular in both Canada and Scotland, that involves a broom?**

a. ice hockey
b. lacrosse
c. sweeping
d. curling

4 **True or false?** In Afghanistan, the sport of kite fighting involves cutting your opponents' kite strings so that your kite can fly the highest and longest.

5 **The tropical island nation of Jamaica surprised the world when it took part in what sport in the 1988 Winter Olympics?**

a. swimming
b. running
c. bobsledding
d. water polo

6 The world's heaviest sumo wrestler weighed 630 pounds (287 kg). That's almost as heavy as a male ______.

a.

brown bear

b.

sheep

c.
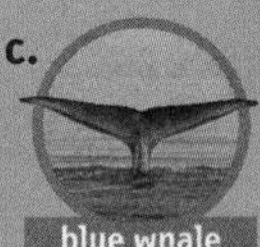
blue wnale

d.

golden retriever

CHECK YOUR ANSWERS ON PAGES 54-55.

7. There are ten different sports in a decathlon. Which of the following is not a decathlon sport?

a. long jump
b. pole vault
c. marathon
d. javelin throw

8. Which American football team won the first ever Super Bowl, played in 1967?

a. Green Bay Packers
b. Dallas Cowboys
c. New Orleans Saints
d. Kansas City Chiefs

9. This skateboarder, nick-named "The Birdman," was the first ever to land a trick called the 900—that's two and a half turns in the air!

a. Shaun White
b. Andy Macdonald
c. Tony Hawk
d. Ryan Sheckler

10. Which country has won the most Olympic medals?

a. Italy
b. United States
c. Germany
d. Greece

11. What is the name of the instrument that fans could be heard blowing during the 2010 FIFA World Cup?

a. harmonica
b. bullhorn
c. trumpet
d. vuvuzela

12. **True or false?** In Malaysia, some athletes play tennis using their legs and feet instead of racquets.

TRUE or FALSE?

Dream Vacations

1 YOU'D HAVE TO CLIMB 354 STEPS TO REACH THE TOP OF THE STATUE OF LIBERTY.

2 IN SWEDEN, YOU CAN STAY IN A HOTEL MADE OF ICE.

3 *ALOHA* MEANS "HELLO" AND "GOODBYE" IN THE HAWAIIAN LANGUAGE.

4 SIX FLAGS DOES *NOT* HAVE A SITE IN FLORIDA, U.S.A.

5 IF YOU WERE IN JAPAN, YOU WOULD PAY FOR YOUR MEAL WITH A EURO.

6 THE FAMOUS CLOCK TOWER IN LONDON, ENGLAND, IS NICKNAMED "BIG BEN."

7 THE LEANING TOWER IN PISA, ITALY, BEGAN TO TILT BEFORE CONSTRUCTION OF THE BUILDING HAD EVEN BEEN COMPLETED.

8 THE CHEESEHEAD HAT—A POPULAR SOUVENIR IN WISCONSIN, U.S.A.—WAS FIRST MADE OF REAL CHEDDAR CHEESE.

9 LAS VEGAS IS HOME TO A GROUP OF SKYDIVING ELVIS IMPERSONATORS CALLED THE "FLYING ELVI."

10 AN IMAGE OF A JAGUAR APPEARS ON CANADA'S MONEY.

11 JAPAN IS HOME TO THE WORLD'S LARGEST FISH MARKET.

12 THERE'S A HOTEL MADE ENTIRELY OF SAND IN WEYMOUTH BEACH IN ENGLAND, U.K.

13 THE WORLD'S BIGGEST FOOD FIGHT TAKES PLACE EACH SUMMER IN SPAIN.

14 STONEHENGE, A PREHISTORIC STONE MONUMENT IN ENGLAND, U.K., WAS USED AS A CLOCK WHEN IT WAS FIRST BUILT.

15 THERE'S A TOILET-SHAPED ROCK MONUMENT IN NEW MEXICO, U.S.A.

16 THE WORLD'S MOST EXPENSIVE HOTEL SUITE COSTS $65,000 A NIGHT.

17 LLANFAIRPWLLGWYNGYLLGOGERYCHWYRNDROBWLLLLANTYSILIOGOGOGOCH IS THE NAME OF A VILLAGE IN WALES, U.K.

18 THE FACES OF THREE U.S. PRESIDENTS ARE CHISELED INTO THE SIDE OF MOUNT RUSHMORE IN NORTH DAKOTA, U.S.A.

19 THE WORLD'S TALLEST BRIDGE IS SO HIGH THAT MOTORISTS CAN DRIVE THROUGH THE CLOUDS.

20 THE ITALIAN CITY OF VENICE, WHICH ATTRACTS 20 MILLION TOURISTS EACH YEAR, IS SLOWLY SINKING.

21 DISNEYLAND IN CALIFORNIA, U.S.A., IS HOME TO THE EPCOT THEME PARK.

22 THE GREAT BARRIER REEF—A CORAL REEF SYSTEM IN AUSTRALIA—CAN BE SEEN FROM SPACE.

23 THE ORIENT EXPRESS WAS THE NAME OF A PASSENGER TRAIN THAT ORIGINALLY RAN FROM FRANCE TO ROMANIA.

24 CALIFORNIA'S REDWOOD FOREST HAS TREES THAT ARE TALLER THAN THE STATUE OF LIBERTY IN NEW YORK, U.S.A.

25 YOU CAN TAKE A BATH IN A TUB OF RAMEN NOODLES IN JAPAN.

26 LEGEND HAS IT THAT IF YOU KISS THE BLARNEY STONE IN IRELAND, U.K., YOU'LL HAVE THE "GIFT OF GAB."

27 YOU CAN TAKE A VACATION TO THE SOUTH POLE.

28 THE "MONA LISA," LOCATED IN THE LOUVRE MUSEUM IN PARIS, FRANCE, IS CONSIDERED TO BE THE WORLD'S MOST EXPENSIVE PAINTING.

29 THE FAMOUS HOLLYWOOD SIGN IN LOS ANGELES, CALIFORNIA, U.S.A., READ "HOLLYWOODLAND" WHEN IT WAS FIRST CREATED.

30 EVERYTHING IN THE RED SQUARE IN MOSCOW, RUSSIA, IS RED.

CHECK YOUR ANSWERS ON PAGES 54-55.

Around the WORLD

...hly ...TREMES

1. This destination gets more than 52 feet (16 m) of snow each year, making it the snowiest place on Earth.
   - a. the North Pole
   - b. Mount Rainier, Washington, U.S.A.
   - c. Whistler, British Columbia, Canada
   - d. Antarctica

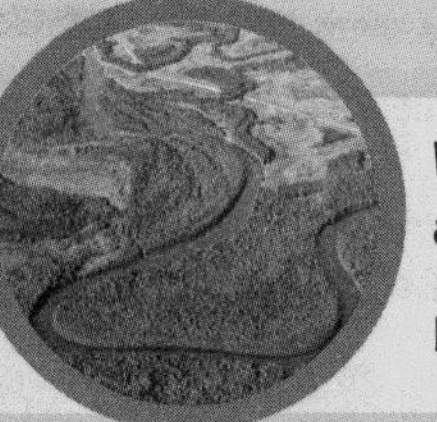

2. What is the world's longest river?
   - a. the Mississippi in the United States
   - b. the Yangtze in China
   - c. the Amazon in South America
   - d. the Nile in Africa

3. In Longyearbyen, Norway—the world's northernmost town—the sun does not rise for how long?
   - a. 24 hours
   - b. one week
   - c. one month
   - d. four months

4. **True or false?** The ocean's deepest trench is deeper than Mount Everest is high.

5. Sandboarders flock to Peru because the country has the world's tallest _____.
   - a. snowbanks
   - b. sand dunes
   - c. waves
   - d. anthills

SAHARA

6 **The hottest known temperature on Earth was recorded in El Azizia, Libya. How hot was it?**

a. 119°F (48°C)
b. 136°F (58°C)
c. 223°F (106°C)
d. 275°F (135°C)

7 **The world's largest desert, the Sahara in Africa, is about the size of _____?**

a. Rome, Italy
b. Puerto Rico
c. the Amazon rain forest
d. Australia

8 **Surfers have been traveling to Nazare, Portugal, to ride some of the world's tallest waves. In 2011, surfer Garrett McNamara rode a wave that was how tall?**

a. 10 feet (3 m)
b. 20 feet (6 m)
c. 50 feet (15 m)
d. 90 feet (27 m)

9 **The world's deepest cave, in Ukraine, is 6,824 feet (2,080 m) from top to bottom. That's about the same as the height of ______.**

a. two Eiffel Towers (Paris, France)
b. the Washington Monument (Washington, D.C., U.S.A.)
c. the Tower of Pisa (Pisa, Italy)
d. five Empire State Buildings (New York, N.Y., U.S.A.)

10 **True or false?** It's impossible to sink in Israel's Dead Sea.

11 **The world's highest waterfall (shown at right) is _____ in Venezuela.**

a. Niagara Falls
b. Iguazu Falls
c. Victoria Falls
d. Angel Falls

CHECK YOUR ANSWERS ON PAGES 54-55.

BE POLITE AROUND THE GLOBE

1 If you want to greet someone in Tibet, you can ____.

a. stick out your tongue
b. brush your hair
c. spin around
d. scream

2 In England, people often do this when they don't like a performer.

a. clap slowly
b. laugh
c. whistle
d. stay in their seats

3 It is customary for people in Morocco to offer their guests what?

a. mint tea
b. handmade rugs
c. pine nuts
d. camels

4 In Bulgaria, which of these gestures means "yes"?

a. nodding your head
b. shaking your head
c. smiling
d. running in place

5 In the Czech Republic, what do wedding guests often throw at a newly married couple?

a. rice
b. peas
c. flowers
d. rocks

6 In Japan, what is it polite to do before entering someone's house?

a. knock on the door three times
b. put on a hat
c. take off your shoes
d. jump up and down

7 In Holland, it is polite to eat your bread in what way?

a. with your hands
b. with chopsticks
c. with a knife and fork
d. with your feet

8 In Indonesia, what body part should you use to point to something?

a. thumb
b. elbow
c. index finger
d. foot

9 People in Switzerland think it's gross to do what in public?

a. speak
b. hold hands
c. chew gum
d. kiss

10 True or false? In China, it is considered rude to eat everything on your plate.

11 True or false? In Turkey, a strong handshake is considered impolite.

12 What number is considered lucky in Italy?

a. 3
b. 7
c. 13
d. 21

13 In what country is it rude to make eye contact when you greet someone?

a. Spain
b. Denmark
c. United States
d. China

14 In Taiwan, it's polite to do what if you enjoyed your meal?

a. rub your belly
b. smile
c. burp
d. take a nap

CHECK YOUR ANSWERS ON PAGES 54-55.

MAP MANIA!

WONDERS OF THE WORLD

1 TAJ MAHAL

Made entirely from white marble, the Taj Mahal was built by the emperor Shah Jahan for what reason?

a. to honor his deceased wife
b. to honor his children
c. to please his king
d. to create a tourist attraction in his country

NORTH AMERICA
MEXICO
A
SOUTH AMERICA
PERU
BRAZIL
B
C

2 COLOSSEUM

The Colosseum is an arena that held up to 50,000 spectators. People often came to watch fierce fighters called _____.

a. Vikings
b. barbarians
c. gladiators
d. avatars

3 CHRIST THE REDEEMER STATUE

What is the name of the mountain on which the Christ the Redeemer statue stands?

a. Mount Everest
b. Kilimanjaro
c. Corcovado
d. Mount Olympus

4 CHICHÉN ITZÁ

At certain times of year, the sunset casts shadows on this famous Mayan pyramid, creating the appearance of what kind of animal slithering down its stairs?

a. jaguar
b. lizard
c. lion
d. snake

You'd have to travel the globe to visit all of the New 7 Wonders of the World, voted on in a worldwide poll. Take this quick tour to find out how much you know about these man-made marvels. Then try to match each one to the correct location on the map.

EUROPE
D
ITALY
JORDAN
E
ASIA
CHINA
G
F
INDIA
AFRICA
AUSTRALIA
ANTARCTICA

5 GREAT WALL

The world's longest structure ever made by humans, the Great Wall stretches about how far?

a. 100 miles (161 km)
b. 1,000 miles (1,609 km)
c. 4,500 miles (7,242 km)
d. 10,000 miles (16,093 km)

6 MACHU PICCHU

True or false? Inca workers moved giant stones up the 7,970-foot-tall (2,429 m) mountain shown below to build Machu Picchu.

7 PETRA

This ancient city is carved into a cliff made of which natural material?

a. ivory
b. sandstone
c. gold
d. diamonds

8-14 THE COUNTRIES HIGHLIGHTED

IN ORANGE ON THE MAP ARE EACH HOME TO ONE OF THESE WONDERS. MATCH EACH WONDER TO THE RED MARKER THAT SHOWS ITS CORRECT LOCATION.

CHECK YOUR ANSWERS ON PAGES 54-55.

GAME SHOW

ULTIMATE GLOBAL CHALLENGE

Where can you find this famous building?

a. Moscow, Russia
b. Rome, Italy
c. Sydney, Australia
d. Jerusalem, Israel

Which country has the most people?

a. the United States
b. Russia
c. China
d. Mexico

3

TRUE OR FALSE?

San Francisco's Golden Gate Bridge is painted gold.

There are more countries on this continent than any other.

a. Europe
b. Africa
c. Asia
d. South America

On what holiday is it traditional to eat corned beef and cabbage?

a. Valentine's Day
b. St. Patrick's Day
c. April Fool's Day
d. Thanksgiving

6

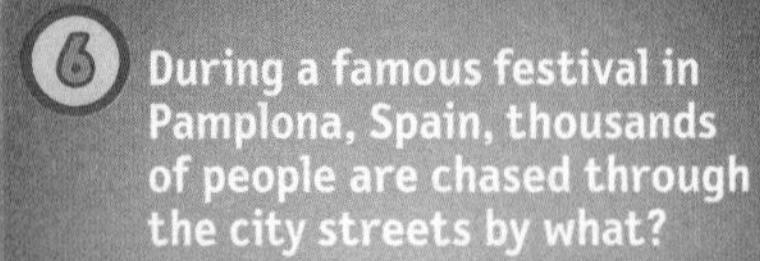

During a famous festival in Pamplona, Spain, thousands of people are chased through the city streets by what?

a. Spanish dancers
b. kangaroos
c. bulls
d. monster trucks

Which skyscraper is the tallest in the world?

a. Taipei 101 in Taipei, Taiwan
b. Petronas Towers in Kuala Lumpur, Malaysia
c. Willis Tower in Chicago, Illinois, U.S.A.
d. Burj Khalifa, in Dubai, United Arab Emirates

8 "The Big Apple" is a nickname for which city?

a. Moscow, Russia
b. New York, New York, U.S.A.
c. London, England, U.K.
d. Hong Kong, China

9 Neuschwanstein Castle in Bavaria, Germany, was the inspiration for which of these storybook locations?

a. Hogwarts School of Witchcraft and Wizardry
b. Sleeping Beauty Castle in Disneyland
c. Dracula's Castle
d. Emerald City in the Wizard of Oz

10 What sport was invented in Scotland?

a. baseball
b. basketball
c. snowboarding
d. golf

11 The hundred highest mountains in the world are all on which continent?

a. North America
b. Africa
c. Asia
d. Antarctica

12 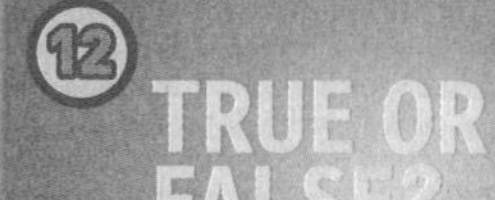

There is a heart-shaped coral reef in Australia.

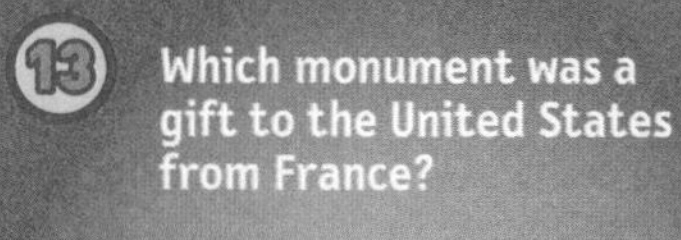

a. 
Statue of Liberty

b. 
Lincoln Memorial

c. 
Iwo Jima Monument

d. 

Paul Bunyan Statue

14 Which of the following would you not see in Amsterdam, Holland?

a. tulips
b. windmills
c. canals
d. a mountain range

15 ULTIMATE BRAIN BUSTER

IN WHICH OF THESE FAMOUS PLACES DOES THE QUEEN OF ENGLAND LIVE?

a. St. Basil's Cathedral

b. 
White House

c. 
Buckingham Palace

d. 
Tower Bridge

CHECK YOUR ANSWERS ON PAGES 54-55.

ANSWERS

Happy Holidays!, pages 36-37

1. **False.** Chinese New Year can take place in January or February, because it's based on the Chinese, or *Yin*, calendar.
2. **a**
3. **True.** At the annual Monkey Buffet Festival, the people of Lopburi, Thailand, honor 2,000 long-tailed macaques that live nearby. Local believe the monkeys bring good fortune.
4. **d**
5. **c**
6. **False.** A shamrock is a three-leaf clover, a shape often worn as a symbol of Ireland. A four-leaf clover is said to bring good luck.
7. **d**
8. **a**
9. **a**
10. **a**
11. **d**
12. **c**
13. **c**
14. **d**

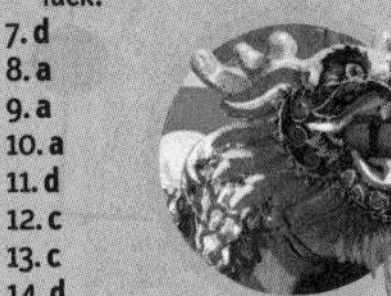

Grand Canyon Adventure, pages 38-39

1. **d**
2. **c**
3. **True.** The canyon is made from sedimentary rocks deposited in layers by wind or water. The bottom layers were the first to be deposited; the top layers were the last.
4. **False.** Native American tribes, including the Hualapi, Havasupai, and Navajo live on reservations in the Grand Canyon.
5. **a**
6. **c**
7. **c**
8. **d**
9. **c**
10. **d**
11. **b**
12. **d**
13. **True.** Some layers are made of sand, lime, or mud that hardened into rock.
14. **a**
15. **b**

What's on the Menu? pages 40-41

1. **True.** Deep-fried scorpions sprinkled with spices are considered a delicacy in China.
2. **b**
3. **d**
4. **a**
5. **d**
6. **b**
7. **False.** Swiss cheese is actually made in the United States and Canada. It resembles a cheese from Switzerland called Emmentaler.
8. **True.** The first pizza was served to Queen Margherita of Italy. It was made with white cheese, green basil, and red tomato.

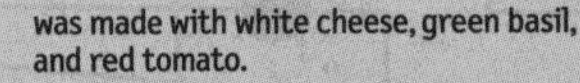

9. **c**
10. **b**
11. **c**
12. **d**

The Wide World of Sports, pages 42-43

1. **d**
2. **True.** Blue represents Europe, yellow represents Asia, black represents Africa, green represents Oceania, and red represents the Americas.

3. **d**
4. **True.** Players use sharp objects in their kites to cut their opponents' kite strings.
5. **c**
6. **a**
7. **c**
8. **a**
9. **c**
10. **b**
11. **d**
12. **True.** In Malaysia, "foot tennis" involves passing a ball across a net using the feet, knees, and thighs.

True or False? Dream Vacations, pages 44-45

1. **True.** If you're up for the climb, you can check out the view from the statue's crown.
2. **True.** Sweden's Icehotel even has beds made of ice and snow.
3. **True.** "Aloha" has many different meanings in Hawaiian.
4. **True.** However, Disney, SeaWorld, and Universal Studios do have theme parks in Florida.
5. **False.** The yen is the currency of Japan.
6. **False.** The nickname actually refers to the 13.5-ton bell inside the clock tower, not the clock tower itself.
7. **True.** Because the tower had been built on unstable ground, part of it began to lean as workers were beginning construction on the second floor.
8. **False.** The first cheesehead hat was made of couch foam.
9. **True.** In addition to the "Flying Elvi," Las Vegas is home to big Elvises, little Elvises, female Elvises, and Elvis waiters, ministers, and chefs.
10. **False.** Only animals native to Canada appear on Canada's currency—such as the beaver, the caribou, and the polar bear. The jaguar appears on the currency of Brazil, where these big cats live in the wild.
11. **True.** The Tsukiji Market is in Tokyo, Japan. More than 900 vendors sell more than 400 different types of seafood.
12. **True.** Weymouth Beach Sand Castle Hotel is made up of 2,200,000 pounds (1 million kg) of sand.
13. **True.** During a festival called La Tomatina, thousands of people hurl 120 tons of tomatoes at each other in the streets of Buñol, Spain.
14. **False.** No one's really sure why Stonehenge was built. Some researchers think it was either a place of healing or a monument to honor the dead.
15. **True.** Toilet Rock is in City of Rocks State Park in Faywood, New Mexico.
16. **True.** The hotel suite, at the Hotel President Wilson in Geneva, Switzerland, has 12 rooms and costs more than some luxury cars.
17. **True.** The name of the village means "Saint Mary's Church in a hollow of white hazel near the swirling whirlpool of the church of Saint Tysilio with a red cave" in Welsh.
18. **False.** The faces of four U.S. Presidents—George Washington, Abraham Lincoln, Theodore Roosevelt, and Thomas Jefferson—are sculpted into the mountainside.
19. **True.** The roadway of the Millau Viaduct bridge in France is 885 feet (270 m) high.
20. **True.** Venice is built in a lagoon. The city has sunk 10 inches (25 cm) in the last 100 years.
21. **False.** Epcot is located at Walt Disney World in Florida, U.S.A.
22. **True.** The Great Barrier Reef spans 1,600 miles (2,600 km) and is large enough to be seen from the International Space Station.
23. **True.** The train first ran from Paris, France to Giurgiu, Romania.
24. **True.** The forest contains the world's tallest tree, at 379 feet (116 m). The Statue of Liberty is 305 feet (93 m) from base to torch.
25. **True.** A Ramen noodle bath is available to customers at Yunessan Spa in Japan.
26. **True.** Kissing the Blarney Stone is said to make you a great and flattering speaker.
27. **True.** There are no hotels at the South Pole, but you can take a cruise to Antarctica and a guided tour of the pole.
28. **True.** Though the "Mona Lisa" has not been sold, experts say that it is worth more than $670 million.
29. **True.** The sign was created in 1923 as an advertisement for a new housing development. The last four letters were removed in 1949.
30. **False.** The word "red" came from a word that once meant "beautiful" in Russian.

Earthly Extremes, pages 46-47

1. **b**
2. **d**
3. **d**
4. **True.** The Challenger Deep, located in the Mariana Trench in the Pacific Ocean, is almost seven miles (11 km) deep. If Mount Everest were placed inside, there

would still be more than 6,000 feet (1,829 m) of water above it.
5. **b**
6. **b**
7. **d**
8. **d**
9. **d**
10. **True.** The high salt levels in the Dead Sea keep people afloat.
11. **d**

Be Polite Around the Globe, pages 48-49

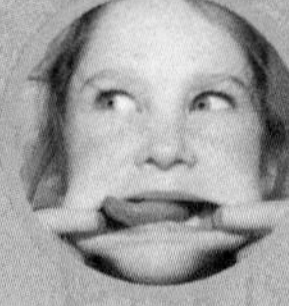

1. **a**
2. **c**
3. **a**
4. **b**
5. **b**
6. **c**
7. **c**
8. **a**
9. **c**
10. **True.** It's considered rude because your host will think that you did not get enough food.
11. **True.** A light handshake is fine, though most people—even in areas of business—kiss each other once on each cheek instead.
12. **c**
13. **d**
14. **c**

Map Mania! Wonders of the World, pages 50-51

1. **a**
2. **c**
3. **c**
4. **d**
5. **c**
6. **True.** Inca workers likely used ropes and levers to move heavy stones up the towering mountain.
7. **b**

Match the Wonder to the Map

8. Taj Mahal-**F-Agra, India**
9. Colosseum-**D-Rome, Italy**
10. Christ the Redeemer Statue-**C-Rio de Janeiro, Brazil**
11. Chichén Itzá-**A-Yucatán, Mexico**
12. Great Wall-**G-stretches an estimated 4,500 miles (7,242 km) across China**
13. Machu Picchu-**B-near Cusco, Peru**
14. Petra-**E-southwest Jordan**

Game Show: Ultimate Global Challenge, pages 52-53

1. **c**
2. **c**
3. **False.** The Golden Gate Bridge is painted "international orange."
4. **b**
5. **b**
6. **c**
7. **d**
8. **b**
9. **b**
10. **d**
11. **c**
12. **True.** Heart Reef is part of Australia's Great Barrier Reef.
13. **a**
14. **d**
15. **c**

SCORING

0-46

THERE'S NO PLACE LIKE HOME

You may feel most comfortable close to home, but you don't have to go far to explore your world. Try international foods, watch travel shows on television, or make a friend who's from another country. You'll learn more about the world and discover places you may want to visit one day.

47-92

TRAVELER IN TRAINING

You are naturally curious about other countries and cultures. Continue to explore, and before you know it you'll be adding the Wonders of the World to your list of dream vacations!

93-137

EXPLORER EXTRAORDINAIRE

You don't like to let your passport gather dust! You just wish you had a bigger allowance so you could hop a plane to anywhere. Let your travel bug be your guide, and one day you might join the ranks of famous explorers such as Ferdinand Magellan and Marco Polo.

Pop Culture

SQUIDWARD (FAR LEFT) AND SPONGEBOB (LEFT) IN *THE SPONGEBOB SQUAREPANTS MOVIE*

Television TRIVIA

1 **Which athlete has *not* appeared on *Dancing With the Stars*?**

a. Hope Solo
b. Apolo Anton Ono
c. LeBron James
d. Shaun White

2 **In what school does the TV show *Glee* take place?**

a. Hollywood Arts High School
b. McKinley High School
c. Ridgeway Junior High
d. Seaview Middle and High School

3 **On *Wizards of Waverly Place*, Alex, Justin, and Max compete to do what?**

a. become the family wizard
b. get the biggest room in the house
c. be the smartest kid in wizardry school
d. do the dishes

CARLY, FREDDIE, AND SAM

4 **What webcast does Carly Shay produce with her friends Sam and Freddie?**

a. iParty
b. iHop
c. iCarly
d. iSpy

5 **The phrase "The tribal council has spoken" can be heard on which television show?**

a. *The Amazing Race*
b. *Survivor*
c. *The Biggest Loser*
d. *America's Next Top Model*

6 **Which celebrity has *not* been an *American Idol* judge?**

a. Jennifer Lopez
b. Paula Abdul
c. Steven Tyler
d. Christina Aguilera

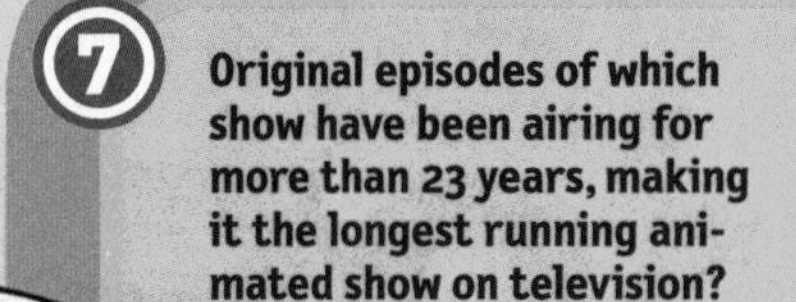

7 **Original episodes of which show have been airing for more than 23 years, making it the longest running animated show on television?**

a. *The Simpsons*
b. *Phineas and Ferb*
c. *Fanboy & Chum Chum*
d. *The Fairly Odd Parents*

8 **Match each host to his correct TV show.**

a. Nick Lachey
b. Jeff Probst
c. Ryan Seacrest
d. Nick Cannon

e. *Survivor*
f. *America's Got Talent*
g. *The Sing-Off*
h. *American Idol*

9 **Which of the following is *not* the name of a Teenage Mutant Ninja Turtle?**

a. Michelangelo
b. Leonardo
c. Raphael
d. Botticelli

10 **Which holiday special has been shown on TV the most years in a row?**

a. *Rudolph the Red-Nosed Reindeer*
b. *It's the Great Pumpkin, Charlie Brown*
c. *Frosty the Snowman*
d. *A Charlie Brown Thanksgiving*

11 ***Planet Sheen* is a spin-off of which show?**

a. *Power Rangers*
b. *Teenage Mutant Ninja Turtles*
c. *The Adventures of Jimmy Neutron: Boy Genius*
d. *Avatar: The Last Airbender*

FROSTY THE SNOWMAN

HANNAH MONTANA

12 **What do Hannah Montana's friends and family call her?**

a. Traci Van Horn
b. Amber Addison
c. Mamaw Ruthie
d. Miley Stewart

13 **Match each character to his or her hometown.**

a. Bart Simpson
b. Clark Kent
c. SpongeBob SquarePants
d. Rachel Berry

e. Lima, Ohio
f. Bikini Bottom
g. Smallville, Kansas
h. Springfield

CHECK YOUR ANSWERS ON PAGES 70-71.

SUPER-HEROES

THOR

IRON MAN

SPIDER-MAN

SPIDER-WOMAN

HAWKEYE

WOLVERINE

CAPTAIN AMERICA

THE AVENGERS COMIC BOOK CHARACTERS

1. **True or false?** Captain America uses his shield as a throwing weapon.

2. **Captain America wears a mask to hide his true identity. Who is Captain America?**
   - **a.** Matt Murdock
   - **b.** Steve Rogers
   - **c.** Dick Grayson
   - **d.** Scott Summers

3. **How did Captain America become a "Super Soldier"?**
   - **a.** He was given a special serum.
   - **b.** He was born that way.
   - **c.** He trained hard in an Army boot camp.
   - **d.** A radioactive bald eagle bit him.

4. **Hawkeye carries a bow and arrow. How did he learn to be an archer?**
   - **a.** He trained with Robin Hood.
   - **b.** He learned as a carnival performer.
   - **c.** He learned in the military.
   - **d.** He went to an archery school on the planet Krypton.

5. **Before appearing in the movie *The Avengers*, in theaters in 2012, Hawkeye made an appearance in what other superhero movie?**
   - **a.** *Captain America: The First Avenger*
   - **b.** *Iron Man 2*
   - **c.** *Thor*
   - **d.** *The Incredible Hulk*

6. **Spider-Man can shoot webs from his wrists. He uses these webs to do what?**
   - **a.** swing from building to building
   - **b.** snare people and vehicles
   - **c.** blindfold criminals
   - **d.** all of the above

7. **Thor's magical hammer, Mjolnir, can do which of the following?**
   - **a.** smash things
   - **b.** change the weather
   - **c.** open portals to other dimensions
   - **d.** all of the above

8. **Thor is based on which character in mythology?**
   - **a.** the Norse god of thunder
   - **b.** the Greek god of music
   - **c.** the Roman god of war
   - **d.** the Egyptian god of cats

9. **What does Iron Man's suit allow him to do?**
   - **a.** fly
   - **b.** have superhuman strength
   - **c.** shoot lasers
   - **d.** all of the above

10. **True or false?** Iron Man shoots lasers from the circle of light in his chest.

11. **What is Iron Man's true identity?**
    - **a.** Peter Parker
    - **b.** Bruce Wayne
    - **c.** Tony Stark
    - **d.** Bruce Banner

12. **Spider-Woman has web extensions on her costume. These extensions allow her to:**
    - **a.** glide through the air
    - **b.** shoot spiderwebs
    - **c.** stick to surfaces
    - **d.** run quickly

13. **What are Wolverine's claws made of?**
    - **a.** bone
    - **b.** metal
    - **c.** plastic
    - **d.** both a and b

14. **What is the name of Wolverine's archenemy?**
    - **a.** The Hulk
    - **b.** Cyclops
    - **c.** Sabretooth
    - **d.** Beast

CHECK YOUR ANSWERS ON PAGES 70-71.

TRUE or FALSE?

Blockbuster Movies!

1. THE CHARACTER PUSS IN BOOTS FIRST APPEARED IN *SHREK FOREVER AFTER.*

2. BUZZ LIGHTYEAR FROM THE *TOY STORY* SERIES IS KNOWN FOR SAYING, "MAY THE FORCE BE WITH YOU!"

3. IN THE MOVIE *AVATAR*, THE NA'VI TRIBE OF BLUE, HUMANLIKE CREATURES LIVE ON A MOON CALLED PINTURA.

4. IN *HIGH SCHOOL MUSICAL*, TROY IS THE STAR OF THE SCHOOL BASKETBALL TEAM.

5. IN THE MOVIE *MARLEY & ME*, MARLEY IS A COLLIE.

6. *BEAUTY AND THE BEAST* TAKES PLACE IN "MONSTROPOLIS."

7. IN THE MOVIE *SPIDER-MAN*, PETER PARKER DEVELOPS SPECIAL POWERS AFTER BEING BITTEN BY A RADIOACTIVE SPIDER.

8. IN *FINDING NEMO*, MARLIN SETS OUT TO FIND HIS SON WITH THE HELP OF ANOTHER FISH NAMED DORY.

9. IN THE FIRST *NIGHT AT THE MUSEUM* MOVIE, PRESIDENT THEODORE "TEDDY" ROOSEVELT HELPS SAVE THE AMERICAN MUSEUM OF NATURAL HISTORY IN WASHINGTON, D.C., U.S.A.

10. IN *GREEN LANTERN*, A DYING ALIEN ASKS HAL JORDAN TO BECOME A MEMBER OF THE ELITE GREEN LANTERN CORPS.

11. IN *HOW TO TRAIN YOUR DRAGON*, HICCUP IS THE SON OF A ROMAN GLADIATOR.

12. *NEW MOON* IS THE FIRST MOVIE IN THE *TWILIGHT* SERIES.

13. THE FIRST MUPPET MOVIE CAME OUT IN THEATERS IN 2011.

14. *THE HUNGER GAMES* WAS A BOOK BEFORE IT BECAME A MOVIE.

15. CROOKSHANKS WAS THE NAME OF HARRY POTTER'S PET OWL.

16 IN *THE INCREDIBLES*, DASH'S SUPERPOWER IS INVISIBILITY.

17 THE MOVIE *BABE* IS ABOUT A PIG THAT WANTS TO BECOME A ROOSTER.

18 CRUELLA DE VIL IS A VILLAIN WHO IS DETERMINED TO HAVE A COAT MADE OF CHIHUAHUA FUR.

19 IN *TITANIC*, THE CHARACTERS JACK AND ROSE ARE BASED ON REAL PEOPLE WHO WERE ABOARD THE SHIP.

20 IN THE *TRANSFORMER* MOVIES, OPTIMUS PRIME IS THE LEADER OF THE AUTOBOTS.

21 BATMAN PROTECTS A FICTIONAL CITY CALLED METROPOLIS.

22 IN *NIGHT AT THE MUSEUM: BATTLE OF THE SMITHSONIAN*, AMELIA EARHART HELPS LARRY THE SECURITY GUARD TRAP JEDEDIAH IN AN HOURGLASS.

23 "MY PRECIOUS!" IS AN EXPRESSION THAT GOLLUM OFTEN USES IN THE *LORD OF THE RINGS* TRILOGY.

24 IN THE *TWILIGHT* MOVIES, BELLA SWAN'S FIRST NAME IS REALLY ISABELLA.

25 IN *THE POLAR EXPRESS*, A YOUNG BOY TAKES A TRAIN TO ANTARCTICA.

26 IN THE MOVIE *UP*, CARL GETS HIS HOUSE TO FLY BY ATTACHING THOUSANDS OF BALLOONS TO IT.

27 *HUGO* WAS BASED ON A BOOK.

28 IN THE MOVIE *CARS*, LIGHTNING MCQUEEN MUST REPAIR THE ROAD IN A SMALL TOWN CALLED RADIATOR SPRINGS.

29 IN *THE ADVENTURES OF TINTIN*, SUNNY IS THE NAME OF TINTIN'S DOG.

30 IN *X-MEN: THE LAST STAND*, STORM TURNS INTO ANOTHER CHARACTER NAMED PHOENIX.

CHECK YOUR ANSWERS ON PAGES 70-71.

The Celebrity SCOOP

1. **Which celebrity has won the most Nickelodeon Kids' Choice Awards?**
   a. Will Smith
   b. Taylor Lautner
   c. Jack Black
   d. Selena Gomez

2. **_____ is the voice of Donkey from the *Shrek* series.**
   a. Cameron Diaz
   b. Eddie Murphy
   c. Mike Myers
   d. Antonio Banderas

3. **Johnny Depp has played all of the following characters except ___.**
   a. Captain Jack Sparrow
   b. Willy Wonka
   c. Sherlock Holmes
   d. The Mad Hatter

4. **True or false?** Cedric Diggory was the first kid to die in the *Harry Potter* series.

5. **Justin Bieber's first hit single was __.**
   a. "One Time"
   b. "Eenie Meenie"
   c. "Baby"
   d. "Somebody to Love"

6. **Which soccer star moved to the United States to play for the Los Angeles Galaxy in 2007?**
   a. Cristiano Ronaldo
   b. David Beckham
   c. Thierry Henry
   d. Lionel Messi

JUSTIN BIEBER

JOHNNY DEPP

7 **Which celebrity did *not* star in a Disney TV show?**

a. Selena Gomez
b. Christina Aguilera
c. Rihanna
d. Ashley Tisdale

What does Lady Gaga call her fans?

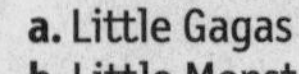

a. Little Gagas
b. Little Monsters
c. Little Giants
d. Little Screamers

9 **Who was the first winner on *American Idol*?**

a. Kelly Clarkson
b. Carrie Underwood
c. Chris Daughtry
d. Jennifer Hudson

10 **Which superstar athlete is known as "The Flying Tomato"?**

a. Tony Hawk
b. Shaun White
c. Apolo Anton Ono
d. Michael Phelps

KATY PERRY

Which famous singer was the voice of Smurfette in the movie *The Smurfs?*

a. Taylor Swift
b. Beyoncé
c. Katy Perry
d. Miley Cyrus

Jaden Smith starred in which remake of a famous movie?

a. *Footloose*
b. *The Karate Kid*
c. *Freaky Friday*
d. *Alice in Wonderland*

CHECK YOUR ANSWERS ON PAGES 70-71.

GAME ON!

1 Which character does *not* appear in *Nicktoons MLB*?

a. Aang
b. Patrick Star
c. Mickey Mouse
d. Sheen Estevez

2 In the *Legend of Zelda* video games, the number of lives a player has is usually represented by what?

a. hearts
b. diamonds
c. swords
d. bananas

3 In which video game would you find athlete Kobe Bryant?

a. *Madden NFL 12*
b. *NBA 2K12*
c. *FIFA Soccer12*
d. *Mario & Sonic at the London 2012 Olympics Games*

4 Which of the following songs can you play in *Guitar Hero World Tour*?

a. "Baby" by Justin Bieber
b. "You Belong With Me" by Taylor Swift
c. "Who Says" by Selena Gomez and the Scene
d. "Livin' on a Prayer" by Bon Jovi

5 Which Nintendo video game character is a friend of Mario and Luigi?

a. Bowser
b. Zelda
c. Princess Peach
d. Donkey Kong

6 Why are the Angry Birds so angry?

a. Their eggs have been stolen by green pigs.
b. They haven't gotten much sleep.
c. Their nests have been destroyed by aliens.
d. Their food has been eaten by a pink dinosaur.

7 Which of the following sports is *not* part of *Wii Sports Resort*?

a. wakeboarding
b. basketball
c. volleyball
d. Frisbee

8 True or false? The object of *Tetris* is to zap as many aliens as possible.

9 Which of the following characters is *not* a video game villain?

a. Ganon
b. Donkey Kong
c. Dr. Robotnik
d. Link

10 Match each of the following characters to the vintage video game it belongs in.

a. alien
b. crocodile
c. frog
d. ghost
e. *Pac-Man*
f. *Space Invaders*
g. *Pitfall*
h. *Frogger*

11 "Sweat," "Duet," and "Simon Says" are all modes of which video game?

a. *Wii Fit*
b. *Just Dance 3*
c. *Rockstar*
d. *American Idol*

12 Which famous movie series inspired a Lego video game?

a. *Indiana Jones*
b. *Star Wars*
c. *Harry Potter*
d. all of the above

13 In *Cut the Rope*, players must maneuver what kind of food into the mouth of "Om Nom" the monster?

a. a piece of candy
b. a carrot
c. a ham sandwich
d. a cookie

14 Which of these video game consoles came first?

a. Nintendo 64
b. PlayStation 2
c. Xbox 360
d. Atari 2600

CHECK YOUR ANSWERS ON PAGES 70-71.

GAME SHOW ULTIMATE POP CULTURE CHALLENGE

1 What's the most popular dish at this cartoon restaurant?

a. Krabby Patties
b. Filet-O-Fish
c. fish and chips
d. linguini in clam sauce

2 Which race car driver became the first woman to win the IndyCar series?

a. Melanie Troxel
b. Danica Patrick
c. Milka Duno
d. Ashley Force

3 In the Diary of a Wimpy Kid book series, what is the name of Greg Heffley's older brother?

a. Rowley
b. Jeff
c. Rodrick
d. Manny

4 What was the most visited website in 2011?

a. Facebook
b. Google
c. Twitter
d. Wikipedia

5 What is Captain Underpants's real identity?

a. Mr. Benny Krupp
b. Jerome Horwitz
c. Melvin Sneedly
d. George Beard

6 Where does this TV family live?

a. Diagon Alley
b. Waverly Place
c. Springfield
d. Bedrock

7 Rebecca Black became a hit on YouTube with which song?

a. "Just Dance"
b. "Party Rock Anthem"
c. "Friday"
d. "Teenage Dream"

8 Which of these athletes is named after a type of steak that his parents saw on a menu?

a. 
Roger Federer

b. 
Shaquille O'Neal

c. 
Michael Phelps

d. 
Kobe Bryant

9 The Mirror Ball trophy is awarded to the winner of which show?

a. *The Voice*
b. *X-Factor*
c. *Dancing With the Stars*
d. *Minute to Win It*

10 What was the most searched word on Yahoo! in 2011?

a. iPhone
b. earthquake
c. Obama
d. baseball

11 Which of these emoticons was the first to be used online?

a. :-)
b. :-I
c. <3
d. >:-(

12 ULTIMATE BRAIN BUSTER

WHICH OF THESE *TOY STORY* CHARACTERS WAS THE FIRST TOY EVER TO BE ADVERTISED ON TELEVISION?

a. 
Woody

b. 
Mr. Potato Head

c. 
Barbie

d. 
Toy Soldiers

CHECK YOUR ANSWERS ON PAGES 70-71.

ANSWERS

Television Trivia, pages 58-59

1. c
2. b
3. a
4. c
5. b
6. d
7. a
8. a-g, b-e, c-h, d-f
9. d
10. a
11. c
12. d
13. a-h, b-g, c-f, d-e

Superheroes, pages 60-61

1. **True.** The shield not only absorbs energy, but its disk shape makes it the perfect throwing weapon.
2. b
3. a
4. b
5. c
6. d
7. d
8. a
9. d
10. **False.** The circle of light, called an arc reactor, powers Iron Man's suit and keeps his heart beating.
11. c
12. a
13. d
14. c

True or False? Blockbuster Movies! pages 62-63

1. **False.** The character Puss in Boots has been around for hundreds of years, but his first appearance as a *Shrek* character was in *Shrek 2.*
2. **False.** Buzz Lightyear is known for saying "To infinity and beyond!" The phrase "May the force be with you!" comes from the *Star Wars* movies.
3. **False.** The moon is called Pandora.
4. **True.** Troy is the captain of East High School's basketball team.
5. **False.** Marley is a Labrador retriever.
6. **False.** The movie *Monsters Inc.* takes place in Monstropolis. *Beauty and the Beast* takes place in France.
7. **True.** Peter Parker becomes superstrong, can shoot webs, and climb walls—just like a spider.
8. **True.** Dory is a Pacific Regal Blue Tang fish.
9. **False.** The first *Night at the Museum* movie takes place at the American Museum of Natural History in New York City, N.Y., U.S.A. The sequel, *Battle of the Smithsonian*, takes place in Washington, D.C., U.S.A.
10. **True.** The alien, Abin Sur, uses his ring to find Hal.
11. **False.** Hiccup is the son of a Viking warrior.
12. **False.** *New Moon* is the second movie in the series. The first movie was simply called *Twilight.*
13. **False.** The movie *The Muppets* did come out in 2011, but it was not the first one. The original film, *The Muppet Movie*, was released in 1979.
14. **True.** *The Hunger Games* is the first in a series of books written by Suzanne Collins.
15. **False.** Harry Potter's pet owl is Hedwig. Crookshanks is Hermione's cat.
16. **False.** Dash's superpower is speed. Violet's superpower is invisibility.
17. **False.** *Babe* is about a pig that wants to become a sheepdog.
18. **False.** Cruella De Vil wants a coat made of Dalmatian puppy fur.
19. **False.** Jack and Rose are not based on real people, but some characters are, including passenger Margaret "Molly" Brown, the ship's designer, Thomas Andrews, and Captain Edward John Smith.
20. **True.** Optimus Prime leads a group of transforming robots called Autobots, which battle the Decepticons.
21. **False.** Batman protects Gotham City.
22. **False.** Earhart helps Larry trap evil Pharaoh Kahmunrah's soldiers in a photograph.
23. **True.** A creature named Gollum used this expression to describe the ring.
24. **True.** The character's full name is Isabella Marie Swan.
25. **False.** The Polar Express train takes the boy to the North Pole, where he meets Santa Claus.
26. **True.** The balloons lift Carl's house and help transport him to South America.
27. **True.** The movie was based on the book *The Invention of Hugo Cabret* by Brian Selznick.
28. **True.** Lightning McQueen has to repair the road after he damages it.
29. **False.** Snowy is the name of Tintin's dog.
30. **False.** The character Jean Gray turns into Phoenix.

The Celebrity Scoop, pages 64-65

1. **a**
2. **b**
3. **c**
4. **True.** Cedric Diggory died in *The Goblet of Fire.*
5. **a**
6. **b**
7. **c**
8. **b**
9. **a**
10. **b**
11. **c**
12. **b**

Game On!, pages 66-67

1. **c**
2. **a**
3. **b**
4. **d**
5. **c**
6. **a**
7. **c**
8. **False.** The object of Tetris is to make horizontal rows using different shapes as they fall.
9. **d**
10. **a-f, b-g, c-h, d-e**
11. **b**
12. **d**
13. **a**
14. **d**

Game Show: Ultimate Pop Culture Challenge, pages 68-69

1. **a**
2. **b**
3. **c**
4. **b**
5. **a**
6. **b**
7. **c**
8. **d**
9. **c**
10. **a**
11. **a**
12. **b**

SCORING

0-31

OFF THE AIR

As far as you're concerned, there are more important things in life than celebrities and TV shows. And you're right! You're an individual who doesn't like to follow the crowd. Celebrate being uniquely you!

32-63

IN THE KNOW

You never miss your favorite TV shows or the newest release from your favorite singers. But you're no couch potato. You know that real life can be a lot more interesting than reality TV.

64-95

YOU'RE A SUPERSTAR!

You always have the inside scoop! There isn't a reality show you haven't watched or celebrity gossip you haven't heard. Just be sure to take a break from the TV and computer once in a while, and go outside for some fresh air.

The Great OUTDOORS

YOU LIKE HOW I CHANGED MY COLOR TO MATCH THE PAGE?

CHAMELEON

MEH.
I'LL BE
IMPRESSED
WHEN YOU CAN
SING.
TOUCAN

Pick Your POISON

SEA NETTLE JELLYFISH

1. **What effect can a jellyfish sting have on its prey?**
   a. mild sting
   b. makes it unable to move
   c. death
   d. any of the above, depending on the type of jellyfish and size of the prey

2. **True or false?** Ancient Greeks used bee venom to treat baldness.

3. **Which of the following is the most poisonous to humans?**
   a. dandelion
   b. pine trees
   c. rosary pea
   d. poinsettia

4. **True or false?** Mosquitoes inject poison into your skin.

5. **The venom of a black widow spider is 15 times more deadly than that of a _____.**
   a. honeybee
   b. rattlesnake
   c. salamander
   d. mosquito

HONEYBEE

RATTLESNAKE

SALAMANDER

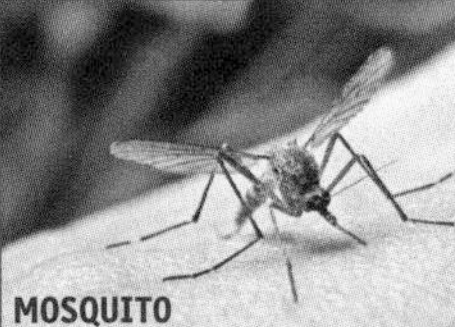
MOSQUITO

6. **Which of these animals is *not* venomous?**
   a. scorpion
   b. stonefish
   c. blue-ringed octopus
   d. vampire bat

7. **True or false?** Daddy longlegs are the most poisonous spiders on Earth, but luckily their fangs are too short to bite humans.

8. **Which endangered animal has a pair of poisonous spurs on the back of its legs?**
   a. koala
   b. jaguar
   c. panda
   d. platypus

9. **True or false?** Salamanders can release poison through their skin.

POISON DART FROG

10. **Where do poison dart frogs live?**
    a. North America
    b. Central and South America
    c. Australia
    d. Antarctica

11. **Touching which poisonous plant will cause your skin to itch?**
    a. poison oak
    b. poison ivy
    c. poison sumac
    d. all of the above

12. **True or false?** Sea slugs use poison to defend themselves.

CHECK YOUR ANSWERS ON PAGES 90-91.

THE SUN AND THE MOON

1 How long does a solar eclipse—when the moon is exactly between the Earth and sun—last?

a. 7 seconds
b. 7 minutes
c. 7 hours
d. 7 days

2 Which city is the sunniest place on Earth?

a. Moscow, Russia
b. Rome, Italy
c. Boston, Massachusetts, U.S.A.
d. Yuma, Arizona, U.S.A.

3 How long does it take light from the sun to travel 92 million miles to Earth?

a. 8 seconds
b. 8 minutes
c. 8 hours
d. 8 days

4 What is the sun?

a. a giant comet
b. a star
c. a planet on fire
d. a space station

5 How many Earths could fit inside the sun?

a. 53
b. 10,000
c. 200,000
d. 1,000,000

6 How long is a day on the sun in Earth time?

a. 2 hours, 26 minutes
b. 10 hours, 30 minutes
c. 100 hours, 20 minutes
d. 609 hours, 7 minutes

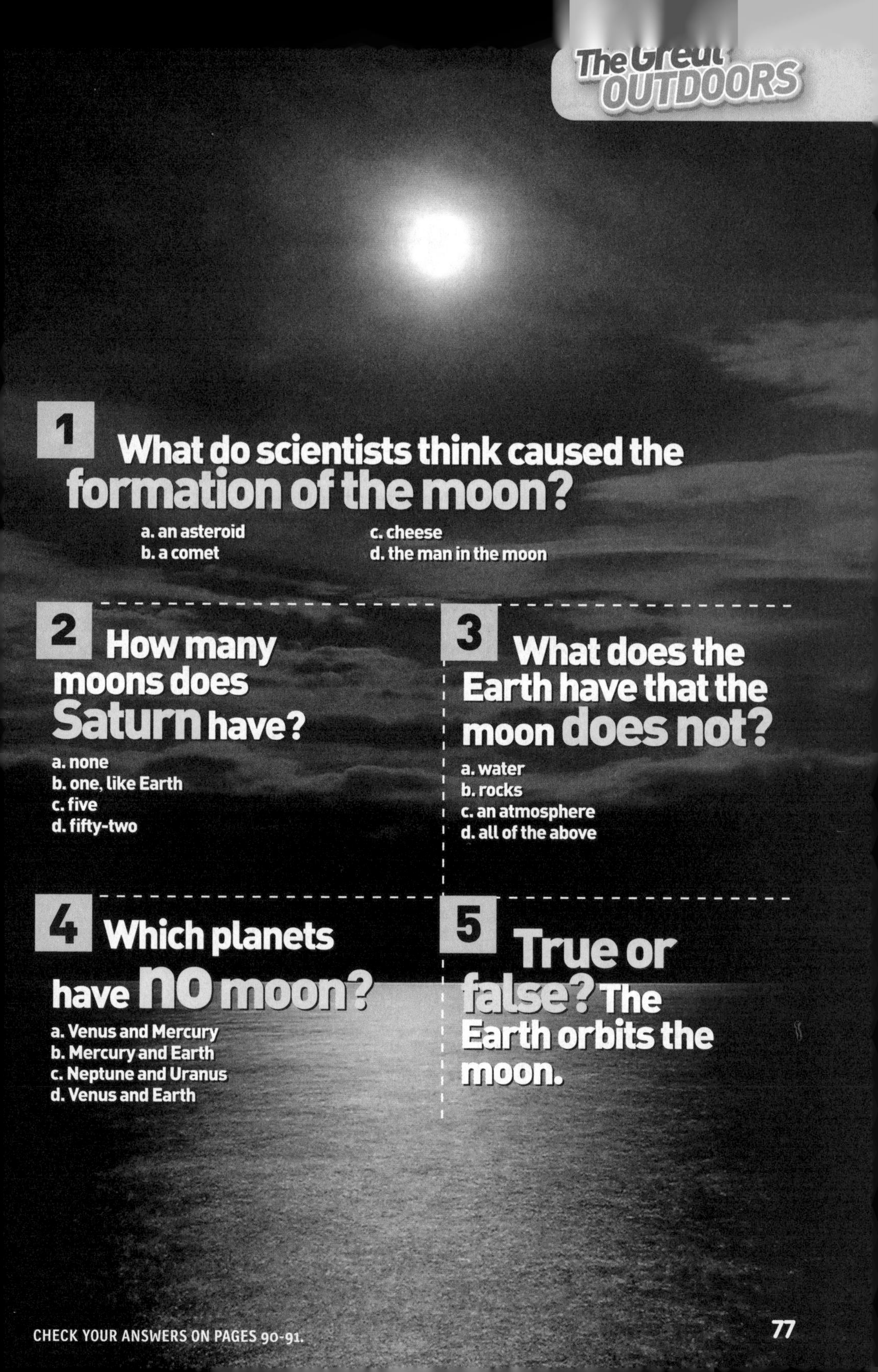

1 What do scientists think caused the formation of the moon?

a. an asteroid
b. a comet
c. cheese
d. the man in the moon

2 How many moons does Saturn have?

a. none
b. one, like Earth
c. five
d. fifty-two

3 What does the Earth have that the moon does not?

a. water
b. rocks
c. an atmosphere
d. all of the above

4 Which planets have no moon?

a. Venus and Mercury
b. Mercury and Earth
c. Neptune and Uranus
d. Venus and Earth

5 True or false? The Earth orbits the moon.

CHECK YOUR ANSWERS ON PAGES 90-91.

Alive in the RAIN FOREST

1. **How many of Earth's plant and animal species live in the world's rain forests?**
   a. one quarter
   b. half
   c. three quarters
   d. all

ORANGUTAN

2. **True or false?** Orangutans swing from tree to tree in the rain forests of Sumatra and Borneo.

3. **How much rain must fall in a forest each year for it to be considered a rain forest?**
   a. more than 6 inches (15 cm)
   b. more than 6 feet (183 cm)
   c. more than 60 feet (18 m)
   d. more than 600 feet (182 m)

HARPY EAGLE

4. **The harpy eagle, found in the rain forests of Central and South America, has talons the size of what?**
   a. a horse's hoof
   b. a dog's paw
   c. a house cat's paw
   d. a grizzly bear's claw

MACAWS BELONG TO THE PARROT FAMILY.

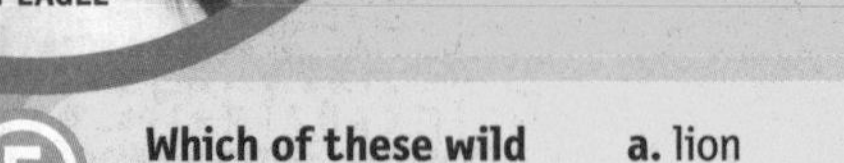

5. **Which of these wild cats prowls the Amazon rain forest?**
   a. lion
   b. jaguar
   c. cheetah
   d. bobcat

6. **Wild parrots, which live in rain forests around the world, can live to be how old?**
   a. 10 years old
   b. 30 years old
   c. 60 years old
   d. 80 years old

7. **True or false?** Amazon river dolphins can be pink.

8. **Banana plants grow in rain forests in India, Australia, Southeast Asia, and South America. How many bananas can grow in a single bunch?**
   - **a.** 5
   - **b.** 10
   - **c.** 50
   - **d.** 150

9. **Rubber trees are native to the South American rain forests, but are now also grown in Southeast Asia and Africa. Which part of the rubber tree is used to make rubber?**
   - **a.** the bark
   - **b.** the sap
   - **c.** the leaves
   - **d.** the roots

10. **Ingredients to make which of the following are found in rain forests?**
    - **a.** coffee
    - **b.** milkshakes
    - **c.** grape juice
    - **d.** all of the above

11. **Which country is home to a third of the world's rain forest?**
    - **a.** New Zealand
    - **b.** Russia
    - **c.** Canada
    - **d.** Brazil

12. **What is the only continent with no rain forests?**
    - **a.** North America
    - **b.** South America
    - **c.** Africa
    - **d.** Antarctica

CHECK YOUR ANSWERS ON PAGES 90-91.

IN YOUR BACKYARD

1 Daisies are found everywhere on Earth except ________.

a. Australia
b. Hawaii
c. Antarctica
d. Japan

2 True or false? Dragonflies can only see straight ahead.

3 True or false? Some ladybugs have stripes instead of spots.

4 Squirrels live all over the world except in which country?

a. Australia
b. Canada
c. England
d. Mexico

5 The American robin can roost in groups of how many in the winter?

a. 250
b. 2,500
c. 250,000
d. 2.5 million

6 What's the best way to provide water to birds?

a. in a bowl on the ground
b. in a bowl in a tree
c. in a water fountain
d. you should not give water to birds

7 A cricket's ears are located near its ________.

a. stomach
b. knees
c. eyes
d. mouth

8 A group of mice is called a ______.

a. gaggle
b. lot
c. swarm
d. mischief

9 At what temperature does sand melt?

a. 3ºF (16ºC)
b. 30ºF (-1ºC)
c. 300ºF (149ºC)
d. 3000ºF (1649ºC)

10 True or false? An earthworm can eat up to one-third its body weight in a day.

11 True or false? A cockroach can live for weeks without its head.

12 True or false? You can fry an egg on a very hot sidewalk.

13 How many ants live on Earth?

a. one million
b. one billion
c. one trillion
d. one quadrillion

14 What is the very first thing a caterpillar eats after it's born?

a. leaves
b. its own eggshell
c. other bugs
d. young caterpillars don't eat

SWALLOWTAIL CATERPILLAR

CHECK YOUR ANSWERS ON PAGES 90-91.

COOL CAVES

1. On average, how long does it take for most caves to get big enough for a person to fit inside?
   a. about 10 years
   b. about 100 years
   c. about 1,000 years
   d. about 100,000 years

2. These icicle-shaped formations form as water drips from the cave ceiling. What are they called?
   a. stalagmites
   b. stalactites
   c. icicles
   d. rocks

3. These pointy formations grow up from the floor where water drops fall. What are they called?
   a. stalagmites
   b. stalactites
   c. totems
   d. chopsticks

4. **True or false?** All bats sleep in caves.

5. Until 1986, miners took what animal with them into caves to test if the air was breathable?
   a. dogs
   b. cats
   c. snakes
   d. canaries

6. Which of these creatures often lives in caves?
   a. glowworm
   b. ostrich
   c. cow
   d. elephant

7. When stalactites and stalagmites touch, they can form what kind of structure?
   a. a column
   b. a big rock
   c. a waterfall
   d. an ice pillar

8. The world's largest cave is located where?
   a. Kentucky, U.S.A.
   b. Venice, Italy
   c. Cairo, Egypt
   d. Antarctica

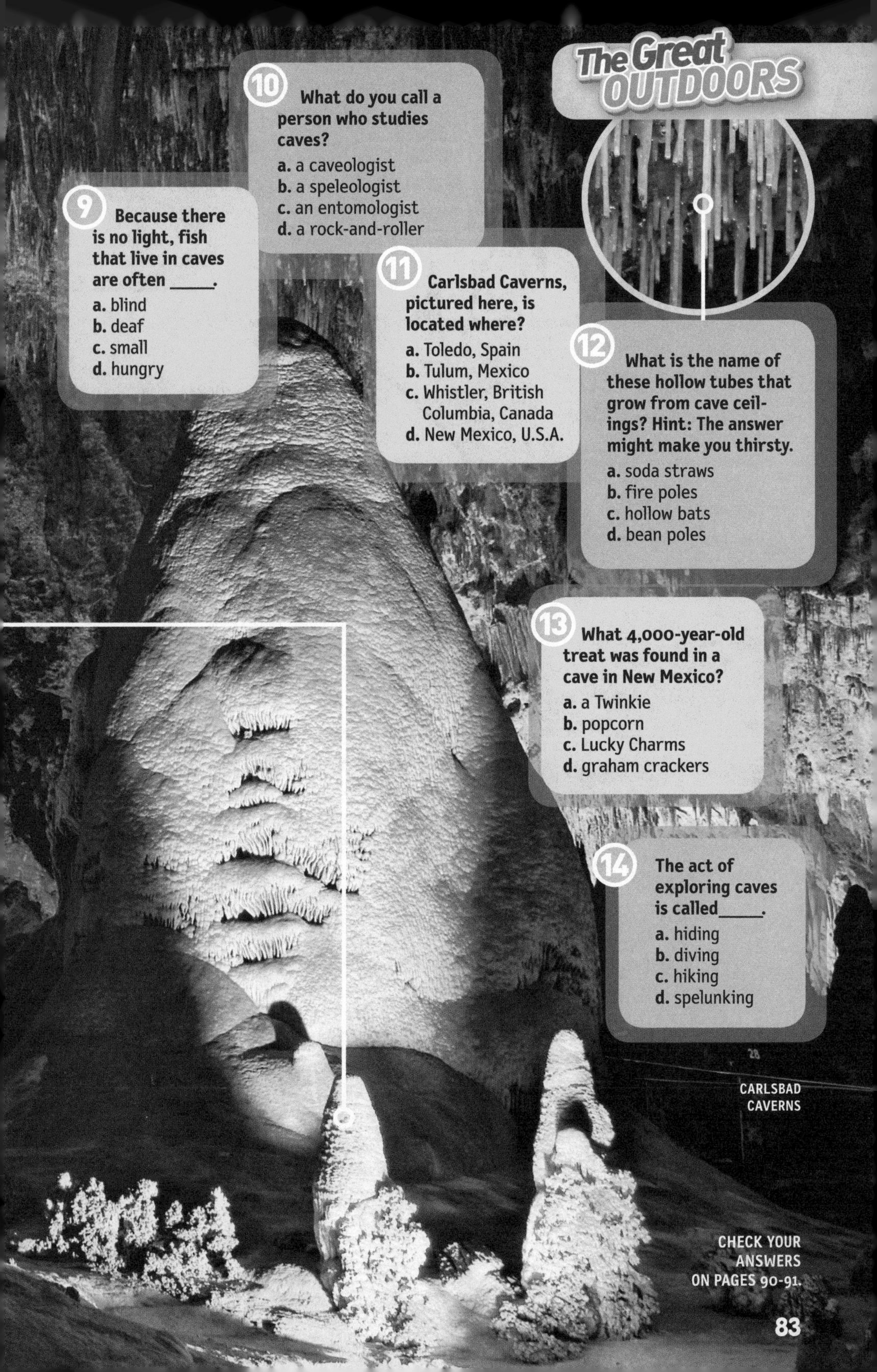

9 Because there is no light, fish that live in caves are often _____.

a. blind
b. deaf
c. small
d. hungry

10 What do you call a person who studies caves?

a. a caveologist
b. a speleologist
c. an entomologist
d. a rock-and-roller

11 Carlsbad Caverns, pictured here, is located where?

a. Toledo, Spain
b. Tulum, Mexico
c. Whistler, British Columbia, Canada
d. New Mexico, U.S.A.

12 What is the name of these hollow tubes that grow from cave ceilings? Hint: The answer might make you thirsty.

a. soda straws
b. fire poles
c. hollow bats
d. bean poles

13 What 4,000-year-old treat was found in a cave in New Mexico?

a. a Twinkie
b. popcorn
c. Lucky Charms
d. graham crackers

14 The act of exploring caves is called_____.

a. hiding
b. diving
c. hiking
d. spelunking

CARLSBAD CAVERNS

CHECK YOUR ANSWERS ON PAGES 90-91.

MAP MANIA!

WONDERS OF NATURE

Match each natural wonder to the red marker on the map that shows its correct location.

ALASKA
A
ALBERTA
B
CANADA
ONTARIO
UNITED KINGDOM
ENG
F
NORTH AMERICA
NEW YORK
D
ARIZONA
C
UNITED STATES
E
Part of Ecuador
SOUTH AMERICA

1 NIAGARA FALLS

2 GREAT BARRIER REEF

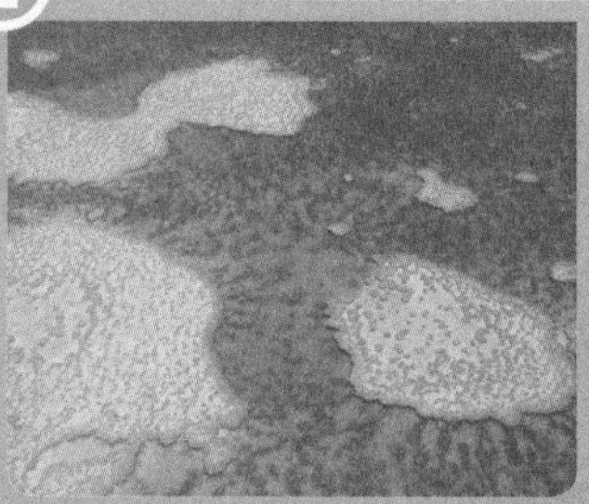

3 GRAND CANYON

4 THE SAHARA

5 MOUNT OLYMPUS

6 DINOSAUR PROVINCIAL PARK

7 WHITE CLIFFS OF DOVER

8 AYERS ROCK

9 GALÁPAGOS ISLANDS

10 MOUNT MCKINLEY

11 DEAD SEA

12 SERENGETI

CHECK YOUR ANSWERS ON PAGES 90-91.

TRUE or FALSE?

Water, Water, Everywhere

1. ALL RAINDROPS ARE SHAPED LIKE TEARDROPS.
2. SOUND MOVES FASTER IN AIR THAN IN WATER.
3. HUMANS CAN LIVE WITHOUT WATER.
4. THE AVERAGE AMERICAN USES 100 GALLONS (379 L) OF WATER EACH DAY.
5. ONLY ONE PERCENT OF THE EARTH'S WATER IS DRINKABLE BY HUMANS.
6. CANYONS ARE NEVER FORMED BY WATER.
7. THERE IS WATER IN THE AIR.
8. THE PLACE WHERE TWO RIVERS COME TOGETHER TO FORM ONE IS CALLED AN OCEAN.
9. THE MISSISSIPPI RIVER FLOWS THROUGH SOUTH AMERICA'S AMAZON RAIN FOREST.
10. THERE ARE MOUNTAINS IN THE OCEAN.
11. EIGHTY PERCENT OF THE EARTH'S SURFACE IS COVERED BY WATER.
12. A PENINSULA IS LAND SURROUNDED BY WATER ON ALL SIDES.
13. WATER IS MADE FROM HYDROGEN AND OXYGEN.
14. LEATHERBACK SEA TURTLES BREATHE WATER.
15. A CAMEL CAN DRINK 500 CUPS (118 L) OF WATER IN TEN MINUTES.

16 A BULL SHARK CAN SURVIVE IN SALT WATER AND FRESH WATER.

17 EARTH IS THE ONLY KNOWN PLANET WITH WATER.

18 AN OCEAN'S TIDES ARE DETERMINED BY THE WIND.

19 FISH IN THE OCEAN DRINK WATER. FRESHWATER FISH DO NOT.

20 WATER BOILS AT 32°F (0°C).

21 THE LONGEST RIVER IN THE UNITED STATES IS THE MISSISSIPPI.

22 CLOUDS ARE MADE OUT OF WATER.

23 A FEAR OF THE OCEAN IS CALLED THALASSOPHOBIA.

24 IT'S DANGEROUS TO BE IN THE WATER DURING A LIGHTNING STORM.

25 EGYPT GETS ABOUT 90 PERCENT OF ITS WATER FROM THE NILE RIVER.

26 THE INDIAN OCEAN IS THE LARGEST OCEAN IN THE WORLD.

27 YOUR BRAIN IS 70 PERCENT WATER.

28 PORCUPINES CAN FLOAT.

29 ENOUGH WATER SPILLS OVER NIAGARA FALLS (ON THE BORDER OF THE UNITED STATES AND CANADA) IN ONE MINUTE TO FILL 50 OLYMPIC-SIZE SWIMMING POOLS.

30 ICEBERGS ARE MADE FROM FRESH WATER.

CHECK YOUR ANSWERS ON PAGES 90-91.

GAME SHOW

ULTIMATE NATURE CHALLENGE

1 The temperature of a typical lightning bolt is hotter than ________.

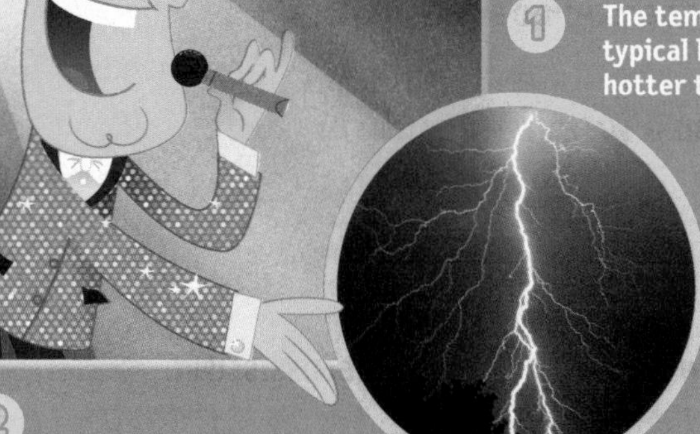

a. the surface of the sun
b. a warm oven
c. a blow dryer
d. a campfire

2

TRUE OR FALSE?
Lightning strikes women more often than men.

You can get sunburned ______.

a. on a sunny day
b. on a cloudy day
c. at night
d. both a and b

TRUE OR FALSE?
A single jungle vine can be as long as seven basketball courts.

What animal can see through its eyelids?

a. horse
b. cat
c. snake
d. mallard duck

This is the funny face of a proboscis monkey. What does proboscis refer to?

a. its big feet
b. its big belly
c. its big nose
d. its long arms

Which of these is called a "bird of paradise"? (You can choose more than one.)

a.

b.

c.

d.

The praying mantid can move only the top part of its _______.

a. arms
b. legs
c. eyes
d. body

About 97 percent of an orangutan's genetic make-up is the same as a human's.

What is the driest continent on Earth?

a. Australia
b. Africa
c. Antarctica
d. Asia

How many species of fish live in the Mississippi River, in the United States?

a. 2000
b. 200
c. 20
d. 2

TRUE OR FALSE?

Worms cannot live on glaciers.

The _________ is the world's smallest mammal.

a. bumblebee bat
b. mouse
c. Chihuahua
d. rabbit

TRUE OR FALSE?

Bats are the only flying mammals.

ULTIMATE BRAIN BUSTER

WHAT AMAZING NATURAL LIGHT SHOW APPEARS IN THIS PHOTOGRAPH?

CHECK YOUR ANSWERS ON PAGES 90-91.

ANSWERS

Pick Your Poison, pages 74-75

1. **d**
2. **True.** Bee venom has been used throughout history to treat many things, from baldness to arthritis.
3. **c**
4. **False.** An allergic reaction to the mosquito's saliva causes the bites to itch, not poison.
5. **b**
6. **d**
7. **False.** There is no evidence that daddy longlegs are poisonous or harmful.
8. **d**
9. **True.** It's their defense mechanism. The poison tastes bad so other animals won't eat them.
10. **b**
11. **d**
12. **True.** Sea slugs eat flowerlike animals called hydroids, which contain stinging cells. Slugs then use the cells to sting their predators.

The Sun and the Moon page 76

1. **b**
2. **d**
3. **b**
4. **b**
5. **d**
6. **d**

page 77

1. **a**
2. **d**
3. **c**
4. **a**
5. **False.** The moon orbits Earth. Earth orbits the sun.

Alive in the Rain Forest, pages 78-79

1. **b**
2. **True.** Orangutans have an arm span of some seven feet (2.1 m), which they rely on to swing through the treetops.
3. **b**
4. **d**
5. **b**
6. **d**
7. **True.** Amazon River dolphins range from gray to bright pink, depending on the clarity of the water. The darker the water, the pinker the dolphin.
8. **d**
9. **b**
10. **a**
11. **d**
12. **d**

In Your Backyard, pages 80-81

1. **c**
2. **False.** Dragonflies' eyes occupy most of their heads, so they can see in all directions except directly behind their heads.
3. **True.** Ladybugs can have stripes, spots, or no markings at all.
4. **a**
5. **c**
6. **c**
7. **b**
8. **d**
9. **d**
10. **True.** Earthworms eat as they burrow, consuming leaves, roots, and other decomposing matter in the soil.
11. **True.** A cockroach does not bleed to death when its head is cut off. Instead the blood clots at the neck, and the bug continues to breathe through little holes in its neck called spiracles. Cockroaches have been known to live for weeks without their heads.
12. **True,** although it's very difficult. The sidewalk would have to reach well over 150°F (66°C).
13. **d**
14. **b**

Cool Caves, pages 82-83

1. **d**
2. **b**
3. **a**
4. **False.** Bats sleep and live in many different places in addition to caves, including forests, cliffs, and buildings.
5. **d**
6. **a**
7. **a**
8. **a**
9. **a**
10. **b**
11. **d**
12. **a**
13. **b**
14. **d**

Map Mania! Wonders of Nature, pages 84-85

1. **d**
2. **l**
3. **c**
4. **i**
5. **g**
6. **b**
7. **f**
8. **k**
9. **e**
10. **a**
11. **h**
12. **j**

True or False? Water, Water, Everywhere, pages 86-87

1. **False.** Although people often draw raindrops to look like teardrops, small raindrops are actually more sphere-shaped, and large drops are shaped like hamburger buns.
2. **False.** Sound moves four times faster in water than in air.
3. **False.** More than three-quarters of the human body is made from water, so we can't live without it.
4. **True.** The water we use to do things such as cook, brush our teeth, and bathe really adds up.
5. **True.** Most of Earth's water is either salt water or ice.
6. **False.** A canyon is a deep valley carved out by erosion from wind, water, or ice.
7. **True.** We can't see it, but there are tiny water molecules in the air we breathe.
8. **False.** When two rivers merge into one, it's called a confluence.
9. **False.** The Mississippi River flows from Minnesota to the Gulf of Mexico. The Amazon River flows through the Amazon rain forest.
10. **True.** There are plateaus and volcanos underwater, too.
11. **True.** Most of this is made up of oceans and polar ice caps.
12. **False.** A peninsula is land surrounded by water on three sides. An island is surrounded by water on all sides.
13. **True.** The chemical formula for water is H_2O, which means it is two parts hydrogen and one part oxygen.
14. **False.** Just like us, these large turtles need air to breathe.
15. **True.** That would be like you drinking about 30 gallons (113 L) of milk at once!
16. **True.** Bull sharks have the ability to keep salt in their bodies, which means they can live in both types of water.
17. **False.** Mars and Venus both have water in their atmospheres.
18. **False.** The gravitational pull of the sun and moon control the ocean's tide.
19. **True.** Freshwater fish absorb water, while ocean fish must drink water to keep from getting dehydrated.

20. **False.** Water boils at 212°F (100°C), except at high altitudes, where the boiling point is lower.
21. **False.** The Missouri River is the longest, at 2,540 miles (4,088 km) long. The Mississippi is 2,340 miles (3,766 km) long.
22. **True.** Clouds are made up of water vapor that condenses, forming tiny water droplets.
23. **True.** Thalasso means "ocean" or "sea" in Greek, and "phobia" means "fear."
24. **True.** Water conducts electricity, so you could get electrocuted if you are in a body of water that gets struck by lightning.
25. **True.** Egypt does not get much rain, so the Nile River is important for the country's survival.
26. **False.** The Pacific Ocean is the largest in the world.
27. **True.** Just like the rest of your body, your brain is mostly made from water.
28. **True.** A porcupine's quills are hollow, so they float easily.
29. **True.** More than 500,000 gallons (1,892,705 L) of water crash down the 18-story-tall waterfall every second.
30. **True.** Icebergs form from fresh water or snow.

Game Show: Ultimate Nature Challenge, pages 88-89

1. **a**
2. **False.** Men are struck by lightning four times more often than women.
3. **d**
4. **True.** Jungle vines can also be as thick as your leg.
5. **c**
6. **c**
7. **a and b**
8. **d**
9. **True.** But chimpanzees share even more DNA with humans—almost 99 percent!
10. **c**
11. **b**
12. **False.** Most worms can't live on glaciers, but annelid worms, or ice worms, do live in this icy environment.
13. **a**
14. **True.** Flying squirrels glide, but bats are the only mammals that truly fly.
15. **The northern lights, also called the aurora borealis,** is a natural light show that occurs in the northernmost places on Earth.

SCORING

0-40

YOU GOTTA GET OUT MORE

OK, so you may be more of a city slicker than a nature buff. It's fine if you prefer to keep your feet on the pavement. But don't forget to check out the plants and animals right in your own backyard. Before long you might be tiptoeing through the tulips.

41-80

ON THE FENCE

You've got nature know-how! Whether you're hiking in the woods or surfing the Web, you're fascinated by the wonders of nature. Every now and then you may get a case of cabin fever. That probably means you need to get outside a little more to explore the great outdoors.

81-120

FORCE OF NATURE!

There's a tornado of nature knowledge spinning around in your head. You probably know the name of every bird, bug, and tree in your neighborhood, and can't wait for your next camping trip so you can learn more. Use your knowledge to help conserve the natural world.

PREPARE TO SEE MY LATEST JOUSTING SKILLS.

Time MACHINE

YEAH, BUT YOUR HELMET IS SO LAST CENTURY.

Funniest Fads OF ALL TIME

1. **Where did the idea for hula hoops, which became a craze in the late 1950s, come from?**
   a. bamboo hoops used by Australian kids
   b. tire rims used by Swedish kids
   c. metal hoops used by construction workers
   d. circular branches used by monkeys

2. **True or false?** Swallowing as many goldfish as possible was once a popular fad among college students.

3. **Stuffing as many people as possible into a ______ became popular in the 1950s.**
   a. mail truck
   b. closet
   c. phone booth
   d. movie theater

4. **In 1924, Alvin "Shipwreck" Kelly started a fad called pole-sitting when he climbed to the top of a flagpole—and sat on it. How long did he sit?**
   a. 30 minutes
   b. 3 hours and 22 minutes
   c. 9 hours
   d. 13 hours and 13 minutes

5. **True or false?** The art of tie-dyeing had been around for thousands of years before tie-dyed T-shirts became popular in the 1960s and 1970s.

6. **In the 1960s, women piled their hair on top of their heads and teased it until it was the shape of a ______, for which this hairstyle was named.**
   a. poodle
   b. beehive
   c. nest
   d. mullet

7. **While listening to friends complain about their unruly pets, Gary Dahl got an idea for a "pet" that would always be obedient and would never need to be walked. What was this pet, which became a top seller in late 1975?**
   a. a pet rock
   b. a cat-dog
   c. a stuffed toy animal
   d. a pet stick

8 **Mood rings, popular in the 1970s, were filled with liquid crystal that changed color with the wearer's body temperature, supposedly reflecting the mood of the ring wearer. Match the ring color to the correct mood.**

- **a.** dark blue
- **b.** green
- **c.** amber
- **d.** black

- **e.** average
- **f.** stressed
- **g.** a little nervous
- **h.** happy

9 **Which dance style took over nightclubs in the 1970s?**

a. breakdancing
b. disco
c. moshing
d. the Twist

10 **During which decade did the Rubik's Cube originally become popular?**

a. the 1930s
b. the 1950s
c. the 1980s
d. the 2000s

11 **During the 1990s, kids collected small stuffed animals called what?**

a. Jumping Jacks
b. Beanie Babies
c. Stuffies
d. Hacky Sacks

RUBIK'S CUBE

12 **In 2009, these colorful rubber bracelets, in shapes such as animals and letters, appeared on wrists everywhere.**

a. Silly Bandz
b. charm bracelets
c. tennis bracelets
d. friendship bracelets

13 **In the 2000s, hundreds of people—communicating by mobile phone—started showing up in public places to do funny things, such as dance or have a pillow fight. What is this fad called?**

a. flash mob
b. crowd craze
c. flocking
d. block party

CHECK YOUR ANSWERS ON PAGES 114-115.

PIRATES' COVE

1 True or false? Pirates attacked other ships to sink them.

2 True or false? Only men were pirates.

3 What did infamous pirate Blackbeard put in his beard to scare sailors on the ships he captured?

a. black dye
b. burning ropes
c. daggers
d. rats

4 In the 17th century, pirates in the Caribbean were also known as what?

a. buccaneers
b. musketeers
c. avatars
d. cosmonauts

5 True or false? Most pirates buried their treasure.

6 If an 18th-century pirate demanded "belly timber," what would he be asking for?

a. wood
b. gold
c. food
d. a new ship

7 What was a "Jolly Roger" in pirate lingo?

a. a happy pirate whose real name was Roger James
b. a pirate ship
c. a candy eaten by pirates
d. a flag flown on a pirate ship

8 A pirate who lost a leg during a sea battle or sailing accident wore an artificial wooden limb called ____.

a. a peg leg
b. a spindle
c. a crutch
d. a tree limb

9 True or false? The character Jack Sparrow from the *Pirates of the Caribbean* movies was based on a real pirate.

10 *Queen Anne's Revenge* was the flagship of which pirate?

a. Black Bart
b. Sam Bellamy
c. Blackbeard
d. Henry Morgan

11 If a pirate ordered his crew to "feed the fish," he wanted them to:

a. throw someone overboard
b. keep an eye on his treasure
c. make dinner
d. feed his pet fish

12 Which of the following were standard pirate punishments?

a. flogging (whipping)
b. marooning (leaving someone on an island alone)
c. keelhauling (pulling someone under the bottom of a ship with a rope)
d. all of the above

13 True or false? Most pirates wore earrings as a fashion statement.

14 An 18th-century pirate would have used which of the following weapons?

a. sword
b. cannon
c. whip
d. all of the above

15 True or false? Some pirates kept parrots onboard their ships.

CHECK YOUR ANSWERS ON PAGES 114-115.

U.S. PRESIDENTS

1. **Which President held office for the longest time?**
   a. Thomas Jefferson
   b. Franklin D. Roosevelt
   c. Richard Nixon
   d. Bill Clinton

2. **Eight U.S. Presidents were born in this state, more than in any other state.**
   a. Massachusetts
   b. Ohio
   c. Virginia
   d. Hawaii

3. **All presidents had other careers before going into politics. Match the U.S. President to his former job.**
   a. actor
   b. tailor
   c. peanut farmer
   d. baseball team owner
   e. Andrew Johnson
   f. Jimmy Carter
   g. George W. Bush
   h. Ronald Reagan

4. **Who has been the tallest U.S. President to date?**
   a. George Washington
   b. Thomas Jefferson
   c. Abraham Lincoln
   d. Barack Obama

5. **True or false?** George Washington had wooden teeth.

ABRAHAM LINCOLN

GEORGE WASHINGTON

6. **The eighth President of the United States, Martin Van Buren, was nicknamed "Old Kinderhook." He was also known for creating which common expression? (Hint: Look at his nickname.)**
   a. LOL
   b. OK
   c. OMG
   d. TMI

7. **Before Theodore Roosevelt gave the White House its name in 1901, what had the President's home been called?**
   a. President's Palace
   b. President's House
   c. Executive Mansion
   d. all of the above

8 **Match the name of the famous first pet to its presidential owner.**

a. Sweetlips
b. Bo
c. King Tut
d. Fuzzy

e. Barack Obama
f. George Washington
g. Ronald Reagan
h. Herbert Hoover

BO THE PORTUGUESE WATER DOG

9 **What is the U.S. President's yearly salary?**

a. $100,000
b. $400,000
c. $750,000
d. $1,000,000

10 **True or false?** Barack Obama is the first African American to be President of the United States.

11 **Known for his sweet tooth, Ronald Reagan kept a large jar of what kind of candy in the Oval Office?**

a. M&M's
b. jelly beans
c. Sour Patch Kids
d. licorice

12 **Who was the first President to live in the White House?**

a. George Washington
b. John Adams
c. James Madison
d. Thomas Jefferson

13 **Abraham Lincoln was known for wearing which type of clothing?**

a. suspenders
b. top hat
c. sneakers
d. wristwatch

14 **What was usually on John F. Kennedy's lunch menu?**

a. New England clam chowder
b. meat loaf
c. grilled cheese sandwich
d. hot dog

15 **What is the President's heli-copter called?**

a. Chopper One
b. Eagle One
c. Marine One
d. Flyer One

CHECK YOUR ANSWERS ON PAGES 114-115.

SINK OR SWIM? TITANIC TRIVIA

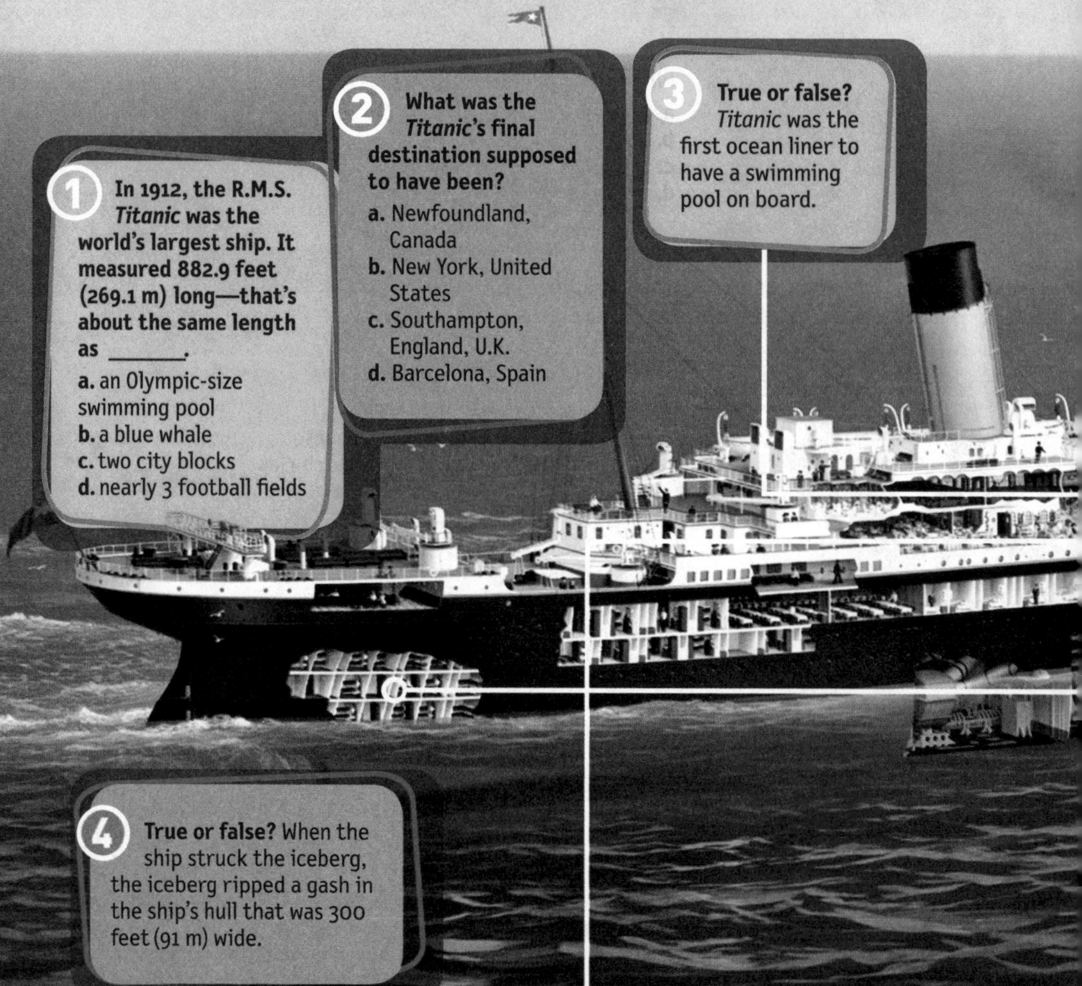

1 **In 1912, the R.M.S. *Titanic* was the world's largest ship. It measured 882.9 feet (269.1 m) long—that's about the same length as _______.**

a. an Olympic-size swimming pool
b. a blue whale
c. two city blocks
d. nearly 3 football fields

2 **What was the *Titanic*'s final destination supposed to have been?**

a. Newfoundland, Canada
b. New York, United States
c. Southampton, England, U.K.
d. Barcelona, Spain

3 **True or false?** *Titanic* was the first ocean liner to have a swimming pool on board.

4 **True or false?** When the ship struck the iceberg, the iceberg ripped a gash in the ship's hull that was 300 feet (91 m) wide.

5 **True or false?** After the *Titanic* crashed, the ship's musicians gathered on deck to play music.

6 **First-class passengers ate in this dining room. Which of the following foods was *not* on their last menu?**

a. creamed carrots
b. lamb with mint sauce
c. roasted squab
d. chicken nuggets

7 **True or false?** The *Titanic*'s passengers had a lifeboat drill on the day the ship struck an iceberg.

8 **As the ship's lookout, Frederick Fleet's job was to stand in the highest point on the ship, called the ________, to scan the ocean for icebergs. He spotted one on April 14 at 11:40 p.m.**

a. head
b. crow's nest
c. engine room
d. mast

9 **Second-class passengers had access to all of the following areas except the _____.**

a. library
b. barber shop
c. deck
d. gymnasium

R.M.S. *TITANIC*

10 **All third-class rooms had running water. However, there were only two _____ for the 710 third-class passengers to share.**

a. chairs
b. pillows
c. bathtubs
d. plates

11 **The bridge was the command center of the ship. Who stood here to give orders to the engineers below?**

a. first-class passengers
b. the captain
c. stewards
d. the chef

12 ***Titanic* was designed to hold 32 lifeboats. But at the time of its voyage, there were only ___ on board.**

a. 10
b. 15
c. 20
d. 30

13 **True or false?** Although *Titanic* had four giant smokestacks, only three worked.

14 **Of the 2,227 people aboard *Titanic*, how many survived?**

a. 3
b. 705
c. 1,000
d. 1,500

CHECK YOUR ANSWERS ON PAGES 114-115.

Just DESSERTS

1. **True or false?** The ancient Olmec people of Central America are believed to have been the first to make chocolate.

2. **2. Which of these ice cream flavors has been the most popular in the United States for more than 200 years?**
   a. chocolate
   b. vanilla
   c. strawberry
   d. Cherry Garcia

3. **The world's biggest cupcake weighed 1,315 pounds (596 kg). That's about as heavy as five _____.**
   a. hippos
   b. dump trucks
   c. baby elephants
   d. cars

4. **Girl Scouts have been selling cookies since 1917. What flavor were the first Girl Scout cookies?**
   a. chocolate chip
   b. Thin Mint
   c. sugar cookies
   d. Samoas

5. **True or false?** In ancient Rome, birthday cakes were usually made only for 50th birthdays.

6. **True or false?** Pumpkin pie was served at the pilgrims' first Thanksgiving.

7. **During the 1904 World's Fair in St. Louis, Missouri, U.S.A., a vendor rolled up a waffle-like pastry, creating one of the world's first _____.**
   a. burritos
   b. ice-cream cones
   c. funnel cakes
   d. wrap sandwiches

8 **True or false?** The name for the graham cracker and chocolate treat called "s'mores" was originally "some mores."

9 **What is the name of the dessert made of sponge cake, ice cream, and meringue?**

a. snowball
b. baked Alaska
c. ice-cream surprise
d. white wonder

10 **Which cartoon character is known for his love of doughnuts?**

a. Mickey Mouse
b. Homer Simpson
c. SpongeBob Squarepants
d. Charlie Brown

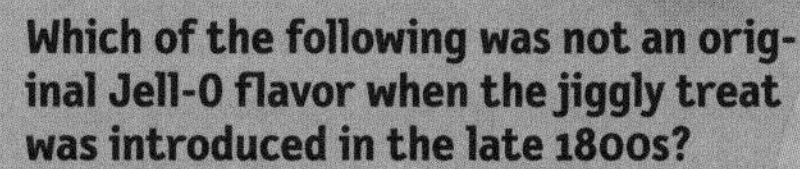

11 **Which of the following was not an original Jell-O flavor when the jiggly treat was introduced in the late 1800s?**

a. orange
b. strawberry
c. lime
d. raspberry

12 **The owner of a bed-and-breakfast called the Toll House Inn is believed to have created the first _____ in the 1930s.**

a. brownie
b. carrot cake
c. chocolate chip cookie
d. cupcake

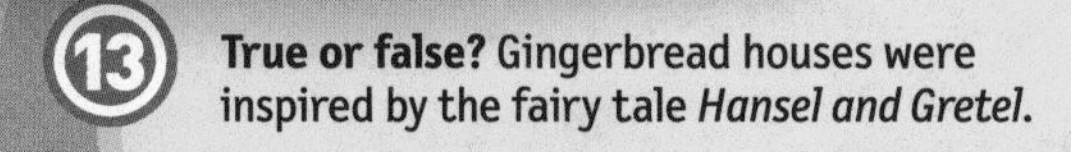

13 **True or false?** Gingerbread houses were inspired by the fairy tale *Hansel and Gretel*.

CHECK YOUR ANSWERS ON PAGES 114-115.

ANCIENT EGYPT

1 To make a **mummy**, ancient Egyptians removed all the organs from the body except the ____.

a. brain
b. heart
c. lungs
d. liver

2 Which one of the following was *not* a **ruler** of ancient Egypt?

a. Tutankhamun
b. Cleopatra
c. Attila the Hun
d. Nefertiti

3 The **Great Sphinx** of Giza—an ancient statue that still exists today—has the head of a human and the body of what animal?

a. cow
b. horse
c. pig
d. lion

4 What is the ancient Egyptian writing system called?

a. Egyptographs
b. cursive
c. Katakana
d. hieroglyphics

5 **True or false?** Some ancient Egyptians mummified their pets.

6 **What title** did many Egyptian rulers use?

a. pharaoh
b. tsar
c. prime minister
d. emperor

7 Ancient Egyptians associated **which animal** with the gods?

a. a cat
b. a rabbit
c. a rattlesnake
d. a crocodile

PYRAMIDS AT GIZA

8 **True or false?** Rulers weren't allowed to show their hair in public.

9 It took about 30,000 workers to build the Great Pyramid at Giza. How long did it take them to build this pyramid?

a. 5 years
b. 10 years
c. 40 years
d. 80 years

10 King Tutankhamun was only nine years old when he became Egypt's ruler. How old was Tut when he died?

a. 10
b. 19
c. 35
d. 50

11 Which dog breed was often used as a hunting dog in Ancient Egypt?

a. poodle
b. greyhound
c. golden retriever
d. Scottish terrier

12 True or false? Men wore makeup in ancient Egypt.

13 The ancient Egyptian civilization was built around what river?

a. Amazon
b. Nile
c. Tiber
d. Danube

14 The scarab was a sacred insect in ancient Egypt. What is a scarab?

a. a mosquito
b. a dung beetle
c. a scorpion
d. an ant

15 True or false? All Egyptian mummies were buried inside tombs.

CHECK YOUR ANSWERS ON PAGES 114-115.

Movie GREATS

SNOW WHITE AND DWARFS

1 **In the classic Disney movie *Snow White and the Seven Dwarfs*, which of the following is *not* one of the seven dwarfs?**

a. Sleepy
b. Happy
c. Grumpy
d. Lazy

2 **The movie *E.T.: The Extra-Terrestrial* is about a boy who tries to help a space alien named E.T. Why does E.T. need help?**

a. He's stranded on Earth and wants to go home.
b. He wants to learn how to ride a bike.
c. He wants to take control of Earth.
d. He needs to come up with a good Halloween costume.

E.T.

3 **Which snack was first served in movie theaters in 1912?**

a. hot dogs
b. Milk Duds
c. popcorn
d. Junior Mints

4 **To watch 3-D movies in the 1950s, people wore glasses that had two colored filters. What were the colors?**

a. black and orange
b. pink and purple
c. blue and red
d. green and brown

5 **What is the title of the book that the movie *Willy Wonka & the Chocolate Factory* is based on?**

a. *Willy Wonka and the Chocolate Factory*
b. *Charlie and the Chocolate Factory*
c. *Veruca Salt and the Chocolate Factory*
d. *Violet and the Chocolate Factory*

6 **In the *Indiana Jones* movies, Dr. Henry "Indiana" Jones travels around the world searching for lost or mysterious objects. What is his job?**

a. pediatrician
b. archaeologist
c. paleontologist
d. zookeeper

7 **Which movie was *not* part of *The Lord of the Rings* trilogy?**

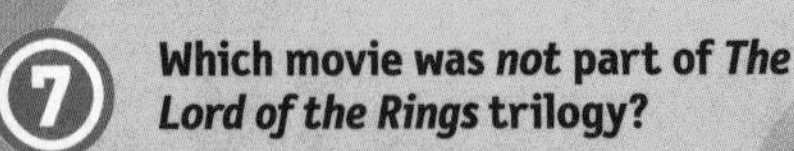

a. *The Fellowship of the Ring*
b. *Attack of the Clones*
c. *The Two Towers*
d. *The Return of the King*

GANDALF FROM *THE LORD OF THE RINGS*

MUFASA WITH CUB SIMBA IN *THE LION KING*

8 **True or false?** The Nickelodeon television network is named after the first cartoon character that ever appeared on the network.

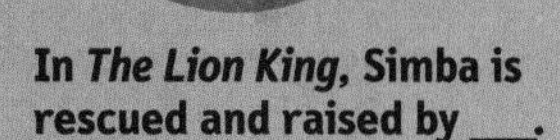

9 **In *The Lion King*, Simba is rescued and raised by ___.**

a. a group of hyenas
b. an elephant
c. humans
d. a meerkat and a warthog

10 **Which famous cartoon character first appeared in the 1928 short movie *Steamboat Willy?***

a. Mickey Mouse
b. Bart Simpson
c. Bugs Bunny
d. Fred Flintstone

11 **In *The Wizard of Oz*, Dorothy Gale lived on a farm located where?**

a. Oz
b. Kansas, U.S.A.
c. Emerald City
d. Cancún, Mexico

12 **The word "Supercalifragilisticexpialidocious" comes from which movie about an unusual nanny (shown above)?**

a. *Nanny McPhee*
b. *Mrs. Doubtfire*
c. *Mary Poppins*
d. *Daddy Day Care*

13 **Which classic movie made people afraid to go in the ocean?**

a. *March of the Penguins*
b. *Finding Nemo*
c. *Jaws*
d. *Free Willy*

KEIKO AND JESSE IN *FREE WILLY*

CHECK YOUR ANSWERS ON PAGES 114-115.

GREEK MYTHOLOGY

1 Where did **Greek Gods** supposedly live?

a. Mount Vesuvius
b. Mount St. Helens
c. Mount Everest
d. Mount Olympus

2 **Zeus**, king of the gods, is often shown with what weapon?

a. a lightning bolt
b. a fireball
c. a shield
d. a spear

3 In the *Percy Jackson and the Olympians* series, Percy learns that he is the son of **Poseidon**, god of the _____.

a. sea
b. trees
c. Earth
d. sky

4 The **Cyclops** is a Greek monster famous for having _____.

a. one eye
b. three ears
c. six legs
d. eight arms

5 **Medusa** is famous for having hair made of _____?

a. worms
b. snakes
c. octopus arms
d. eels

6 True or false? Everything **King Midas** touched turned to water.

7 Which present-day Greek city was named for Athena, the goddess of wisdom?

a. Ionia
b. Athens
c. Kalamata
d. Hydra

PARTHENON IN ATHENS, GREECE

8 The Trojan War, described in a famous Greek myth, was fought over a beautiful woman named _____.

a. Aphrodite
b. Helen of Troy
c. Leda
d. Demeter

9 Which god controlled the underworld?

a. Zeus
b. Hermes
c. Hades
d. Ares

10 Artemis—the goddess of the hunt—is often shown holding a ____.

a. jar of water
b. harp
c. bow and arrow
d. banana

11 True or false? Aphrodite was the queen of the gods.

12 Achilles was a powerful Greek hero who had only one weak spot on his body. What was it?

a. his elbow
b. his neck
c. his knee
d. his heel

CHECK YOUR ANSWERS ON PAGES 114-115.

MAP MANIA!

HISTORY MYSTERIES

Reports of unexplained sightings and events have taken place throughout time. How much do you know about some of the world's most famous mysteries?

NORTH AMERICA
NEVADA
A
UNITED STATES
B
ATLANTIC OCEAN
SOUTH AMERICA

1 ATLANTIS

According to legend, what caused the long-lost city of Atlantis to sink into the ocean?

a. tornadoes
b. earthquakes
c. blizzards
d. an alien invasion

2 LOCH NESS MONSTER

Some 3,000 people have claimed to have seen the dinosaur-like Loch Ness monster swimming in a lake. What are some (unproven) theories about what they really saw?

a. a descendant of a plesiosaur, an ancient marine reptile
b. big waves
c. a large fish called a sturgeon
d. all of the above

3 BERMUDA TRIANGLE

True or false? Giant squid have attacked ships in the Bermuda Triangle.

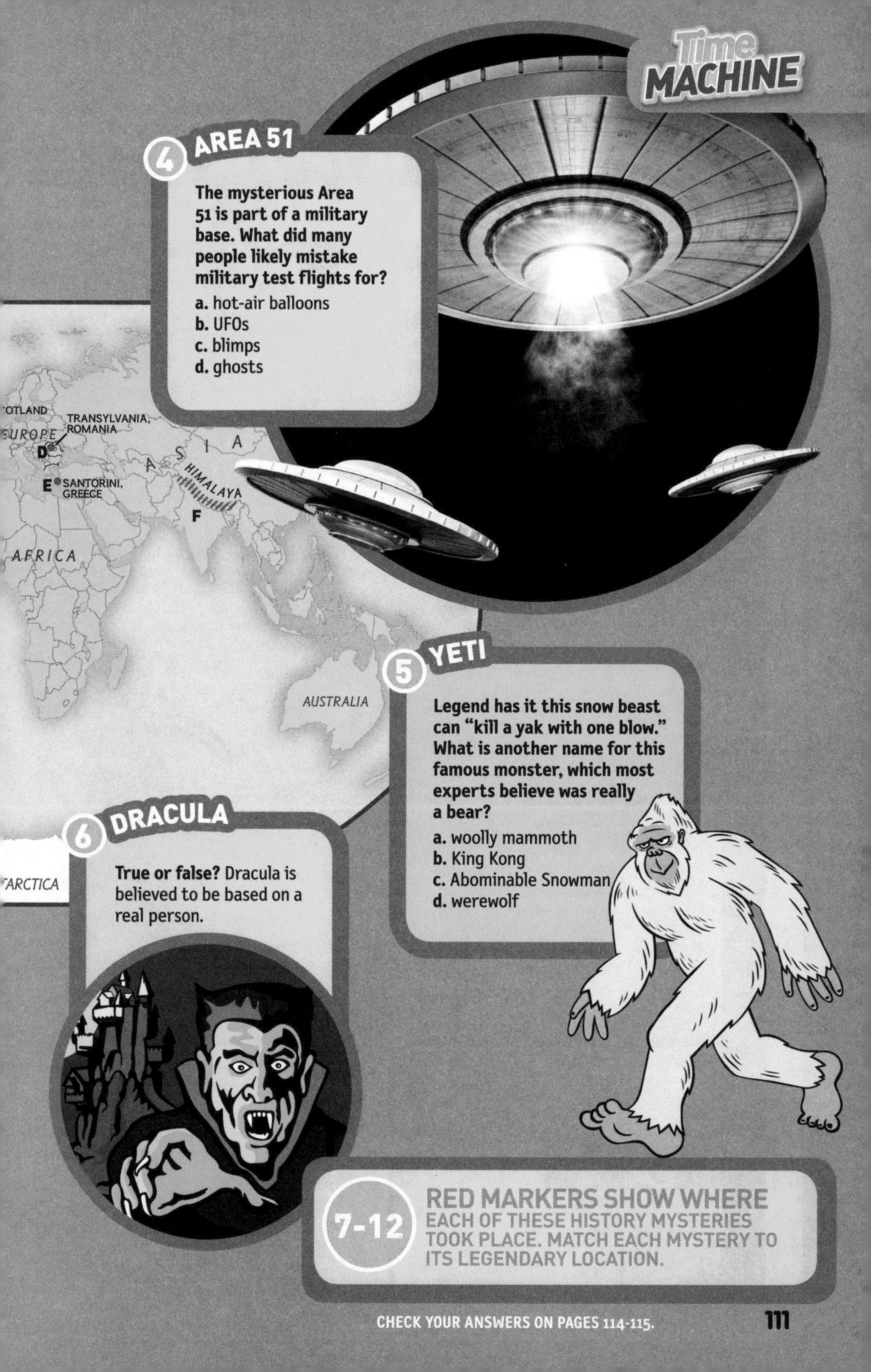

4 AREA 51

The mysterious Area 51 is part of a military base. What did many people likely mistake military test flights for?

a. hot-air balloons
b. UFOs
c. blimps
d. ghosts

5 YETI

Legend has it this snow beast can "kill a yak with one blow." What is another name for this famous monster, which most experts believe was really a bear?

a. woolly mammoth
b. King Kong
c. Abominable Snowman
d. werewolf

6 DRACULA

True or false? Dracula is believed to be based on a real person.

7-12

RED MARKERS SHOW WHERE EACH OF THESE HISTORY MYSTERIES TOOK PLACE. MATCH EACH MYSTERY TO ITS LEGENDARY LOCATION.

CHECK YOUR ANSWERS ON PAGES 114-115.

GAME SHOW

ULTIMATE TIME TRAVEL CHALLENGE

1

TRUE OR FALSE?

The sandwich was named after England's Earl of Sandwich in the 1700s.

2

Which hot-headed superhero appeared in the first Marvel comic book in 1939?

a. Spider-Man
b. Iron Man
c. The Human Torch
d. The Hulk

3

If you saw someone wearing this mask in 14th-century Europe, you'd think he was a ____.

a. doctor
b. actor
c. going to a costume party
d. bird-watcher

4

Jousting was a popular sport for ____ from the 11th century through the 16th century.

a. Vikings
b. knights
c. gladiators
d. barbarians

5

You can read about this teen's wartime experiences in *Diary of a Young Girl*.

a. Anne Frank
b. Joan of Arc
c. Pocahontas
d. Elizabeth I

6

TRUE OR FALSE?

Pennsylvania is *not* spelled on the Liberty Bell the way it is spelled today.

7

Which tasty treat was used as money by U.S. soldiers during World War II?

a. Hershey's chocolate bars
b. frozen pizzas
c. hard-boiled eggs
d. candy apples

8 Which famous landmark was built for an expo celebrating the 100th anniversary of the French Revolution?

a. Mount Rushmore
b. the Eiffel Tower
c. Buckingham Palace
d. Cinderella Castle

9 TRUE OR FALSE?

Today's marathons were inspired by an ancient Greek hero who ran a long distance to deliver a message.

11 Which of these TV families first appeared in a cartoon in a magazine in 1938?

a. 
Addams Family

b. 
Brady Bunch

c. 
Flintstones

d. 
Munsters

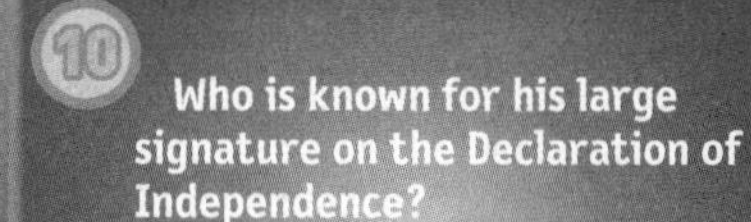

10 Who is known for his large signature on the Declaration of Independence?

a. Benjamin Franklin
b. Thomas Jefferson
c. John Hancock
d. John Adams

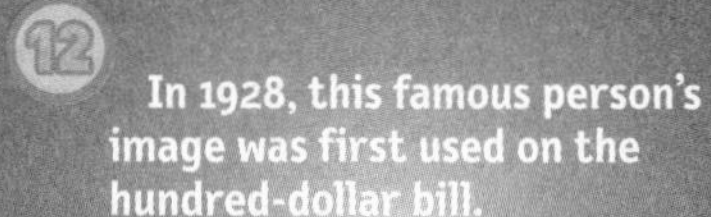

12 In 1928, this famous person's image was first used on the hundred-dollar bill.

a. George Washington
b. Alexander Hamilton
c. Benjamin Franklin
d. Barack Obama

13 Which U.S. baseball team has won the most World Series titles since the championship began in 1903?

a. Boston Red Sox
b. Pittsburgh Pirates
c. New York Yankees
d. Washington Nationals

14 TRUE OR FALSE?

The teddy bear is named after U.S. President Theodore Roosevelt.

15 ULTIMATE BRAIN BUSTER

What classic video game—released in 1978—is shown here?

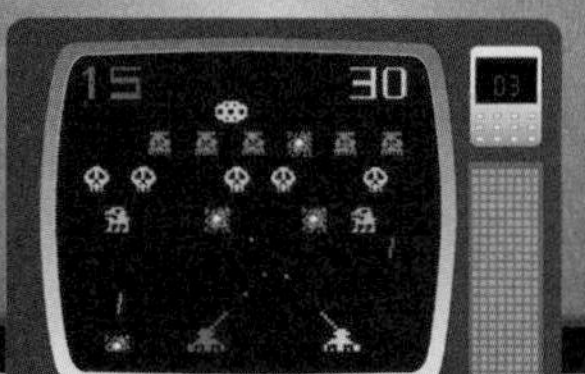

CHECK YOUR ANSWERS ON PAGES 114-115.

ANSWERS

Funniest Fads of All Time, pages 94-95

1. **a**
2. **True.** Swallowing goldfish caught on in 1939. The world-record holder swallowed 300 goldfish in one sitting.
3. **c**
4. **d**
5. **True.** The earliest examples of tie-dye date back to A.D. 500 in an area that is present-day Peru.
6. **b**
7. **a**
8. **a-h, b-e, c-g, d-f**
9. **b**
10. **c**
11. **b**
12. **a**
13. **a**

Pirates' Cove, pages 96-97

1. **False.** Pirates attacked other ships to steal the treasures and weapons on board, and the ship itself.
2. **False.** While most pirates were men, there were a few female outlaws on the high seas. Two of the most famous female pirates were Anne Bonny and Mary Read.
3. **b**
4. **a**
5. **False.** Most pirates spent the treasure they stole. The only pirate known to have buried treasure is William Kidd.
6. **c**
7. **d**
8. **a**
9. **False.** The writers of the movies claim Jack Sparrow was inspired by Bugs Bunny and comedian Groucho Marx.
10. **c**
11. **a**
12. **d**
13. **False.** Pirates believed that earrings helped prevent seasickness by pressing on the earlobes.
14. **d**
15. **True.** Pet parrots were common among pirates who spent time around Central America, where parrots are found in the wild.

U.S. Presidents, pages 98-99

1. **b**
2. **c**
3. **a-h, b-e, c-f, d-g**
4. **c**
5. **False.** Legend has it that George Washington had wooden teeth, but he actually wore dentures made from gold, ivory, lead, and human and animal teeth.
6. **b**
7. **d**
8. **a-f, b-e, c-h, d-g**
9. **b**
10. **True.** Other African Americans have run for the office, but Obama is the first to have been elected.
11. **b**
12. **b**
13. **b**
14. **a**
15. **c**

Sink or Swim? *Titanic* Trivia, pages 100-101

1. **d**
2. **b**
3. **True.** The *Titanic* was the most luxurious ocean liner of its time.
4. **False.** The iceberg ripped open six narrow slits that totaled no more than 12 square feet (1 sq m). Some of the slits were only as wide as a human finger.
5. **True.** The ship's band most likely started playing to calm nervous passengers.
6. **d**
7. **False.** A lifeboat drill had been scheduled, but the ship's captain canceled it for an unknown reason.
8. **b**
9. **d**
10. **c**
11. **b**
12. **c**
13. **True.** Only three of the smokestacks worked. Builders added the fourth because they thought it made the ship look better.
14. **b**

Just Desserts, pages 102-103

1. **True.** The ancient Olmecs, who lived in the southern Gulf of Mexico between 1200 B.C. and 400 B.C., made chocolate from cacao beans.
2. **b**
3. **c**
4. **c**
5. **True.** They were made from honey, flour, cheese, and olive oil.
6. **False.** Although pumpkins may have been present at the first Thanksgiving, ingredients for sugar and crust were not, so there was no pumpkin pie.
7. **b**
8. **True.** The recipe for "some mores" was published in a Girl Scouts cookbook in 1927. No one knows when the name of the treat was shortened to "s'mores."
9. **b**
10. **b**
11. **c**
12. **c**
13. **True.** Gingerbread houses were created in the 1800s after the Brothers Grimm described a house made of candy and cake in *Hansel and Gretel.*

Ancient Egypt, pages 104-105

1. **b**
2. **c**
3. **d**
4. **d**
5. **True.** Wealthy Egyptians mummified pets as a sign of respect, including cats, dogs, birds, and monkeys.
6. **a**
7. **a**
8. **True.** Rulers in ancient Egypt weren't allowed to show their hair. Instead they wore headdresses called nemes.
9. **d**
10. **b**
11. **b**
12. **True.** Both men and women wore makeup in ancient Egypt, originally as protection from the sun.
13. **b**
14. **b**
15. **False.** Some Egyptian mummies have been found buried in the sand.

Movie Greats, pages 106-107

1. **d**
2. **a**
3. **c**
4. **c**
5. **b**
6. **b**
7. **b**
8. **False.** Nickelodeon is named after movie theaters from the early 1900s called Nickelodeons, where people paid a nickel to watch a series of short movies.
9. **d**
10. **a**
11. **b**
12. **c**
13. **c**

Greek Mythology, pages 108-109

1. **d**
2. **a**
3. **a**
4. **a**
5. **b**
6. **False.** Everything King Midas touched turned to gold.
7. **b**
8. **b**
9. **c**
10. **c**
11. **False.** Aphrodite was the goddess of love. The queen of the gods was Hera.
12. **d**

Map Mania! History Mysteries, pages 110-111

1. **b**
2. **d**
3. **False.** Many ships and planes have disappeared in the Bermuda Triangle, but bad weather and strong currents are the likely causes, not giant squid.
4. **b**
5. **c**
6. **True.** Bram Stoker, the author of the book *Dracula*, is believed to have based the character on a real 15th-century prince named Vlad the Impaler. Vlad wasn't a vampire, but he supposedly tortured his enemies and was rumored to have drunk their blood.
7. **Atlantis - E**
8. **Loch Ness monster - C**
9. **Bermuda Triangle - B**
10. **Area 51 - A**
11. **Yeti - F**
12. **Dracula - D**

Game Show: Ultimate Time Travel Challenge, pages 112-113

1. **True.** The food is named after the Earl of Sandwich because he often ate sandwiches while playing card games.
2. **c**
3. **a**
4. **b**
5. **a**
6. **True,** at least by today's standards. When the Liberty Bell was created in 1752, "Pensylvania" was considered a different, but correct, way of spelling Pennsylvania. Today, "Pennsylvania" is the only correct spelling.
7. **a**
8. **b**
9. **True.** After the Greeks defeated the Persians at the Battle of Marathon in 490 B.C., a Greek messenger named Pheidippides ran to Athens to deliver the good news. Unfortunately, he then collapsed and died.
10. **c**
11. **a**
12. **c**
13. **c**
14. **True.** The toy bear was named for Roosevelt after he refused to kill a bear during a hunting trip.
15. **Space Invaders**

SCORING

0-46

STUCK IN THE PRESENT

You live in the moment and may think that the past is *sooo* boring. Try these boredom-busters: Visit a fun museum, learn about the history of your hometown, or ask your grandparents what life was like when they were kids. Pretty soon your short memory will be ancient history.

47-92

RIGHT ON TIME

You really know your stuff! Knowledge about the past can help us understand the present and sometimes hints at what the future holds. Remember to look back every now and then on your journey into the future.

93-138

A TRUE TIME TRAVELER

Congratulations, you've earned the keys to the time machine! You're a true history buff. Follow your passion for the past, and you might become a famous archaeologist or paleontologist. Maybe someday *your* name will appear in the history books.

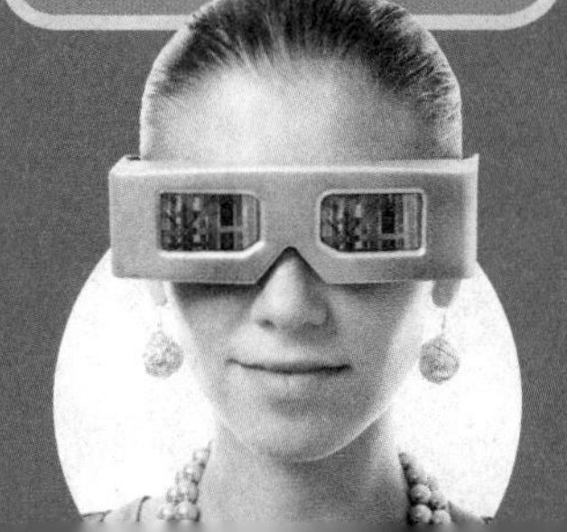

Number CRUNCHER

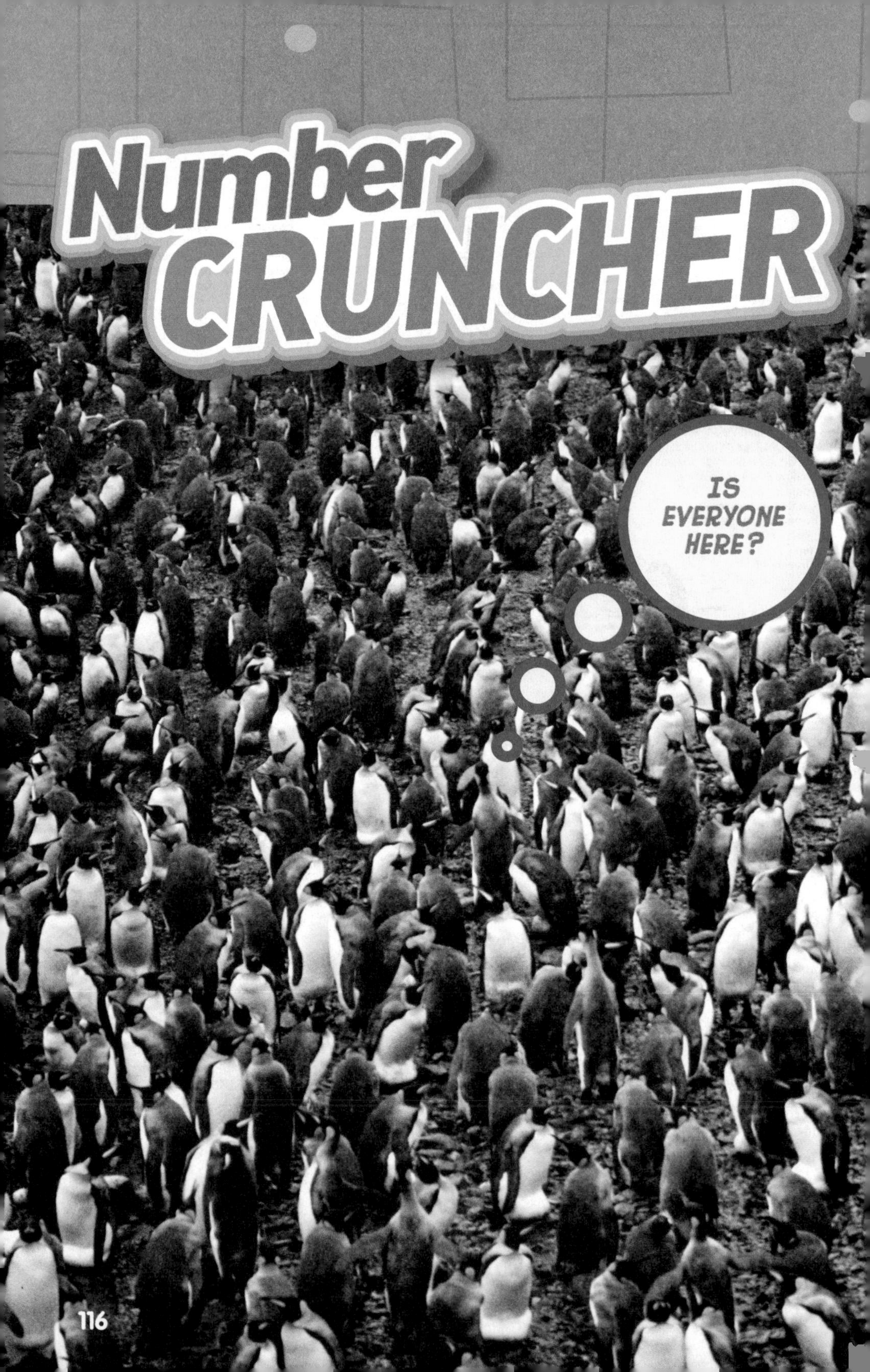

LET'S DO A HEAD COUNT.

Animal FIGURES

How many hearts does an octopus have?

a. 0
b. 1
c. 3
d. 9

The world's oldest tortoise lived to be an estimated ______.

a. 5 years old
b. 50 years old
c. 88 years old
d. 188 years old

GALÁPAGOS TORTOISE

Cats can sleep up to ______ hours a day.

a. 1
b. 3
c. 5
d. 16

The world's smallest cow is the height of a ______.

a. parakeet
b. wolf
c. Great Dane
d. buffalo

How many feathers does an average wild turkey have?

a. 100
b. 3,500
c. 100,000
d. 5 million

About how long does a housefly live if it doesn't get swatted?

a. 1 day
b. 1 month
c. 10 years
d. 100 years

7 **How many dogs are there in the world—"*ruff*-ly" speaking?**

a. 100,000
b. 25 million
c. 400 million
d. 10 billion

8 **A camel doesn't sweat until its body reaches what temperature?**

a. 98.6°F (37°C)
b. 106°F (41°C)
c. 130°F (54°C)
d. 200°F (93°C)

9 **True or false?** Alex, the world's brainiest parrot, could say 150 words.

10 **How many noses does a slug have?**

a. 1
b. 4
c. 15
d. 100

11 **What's the top speed of a sloth—the world's slowest mammal?**

a. 20 miles an hour (32 kph)
b. 10 miles an hour (16 kph)
c. 5 miles an hour (8 kph)
d. less than 1 mile an hour (2 kph)

12 **Which of these animals have been around for 365 million years?**

a. horses
b. kangaroos
c. iguanas
d. cockroaches

YOUNG THREE-TOED SLOTH

CHECK YOUR ANSWERS ON PAGES 132-133.

How the EMPIRE STATE BUILDING Stacks Up

1 **How tall is the Empire State Building?**

a. 54 stories
b. 103 stories
c. 575 stories
d. 1,300 stories

2 **About how many people visit the famous skyscraper each year?**

a. 10,000
b. 1 million
c. 3.5 million
d. 3 billion

3 **About how many times a year does the spire get struck by lightning?**

a. 10
b. 100
c. 1,000
d. 100,000

4 **How long did it take to build the Empire State Building?**

a. a little more than a year
b. 3.5 years
c. about 10 years
d. about 20 years

5 **What year did the Empire State Building first open?**

a. 1931
b. 1972
c. 1995
d. 2010

6 **More than 250 movies have been filmed at the Empire State Building, including which of the following?**

a. *Percy Jackson and the Olympians: The Lightning Thief*
b. *King Kong*
c. *Elf*
d. all of the above

7 **True or false?** On a clear day, you can see 80 miles (129 km) from the building's observation deck.

8 **About how many bricks were used to build the Empire State Building?**

a. 1,000
b. 500,000
c. 10 million
d. 5 billion

CHECK YOUR ANSWERS ON PAGES 132-133.

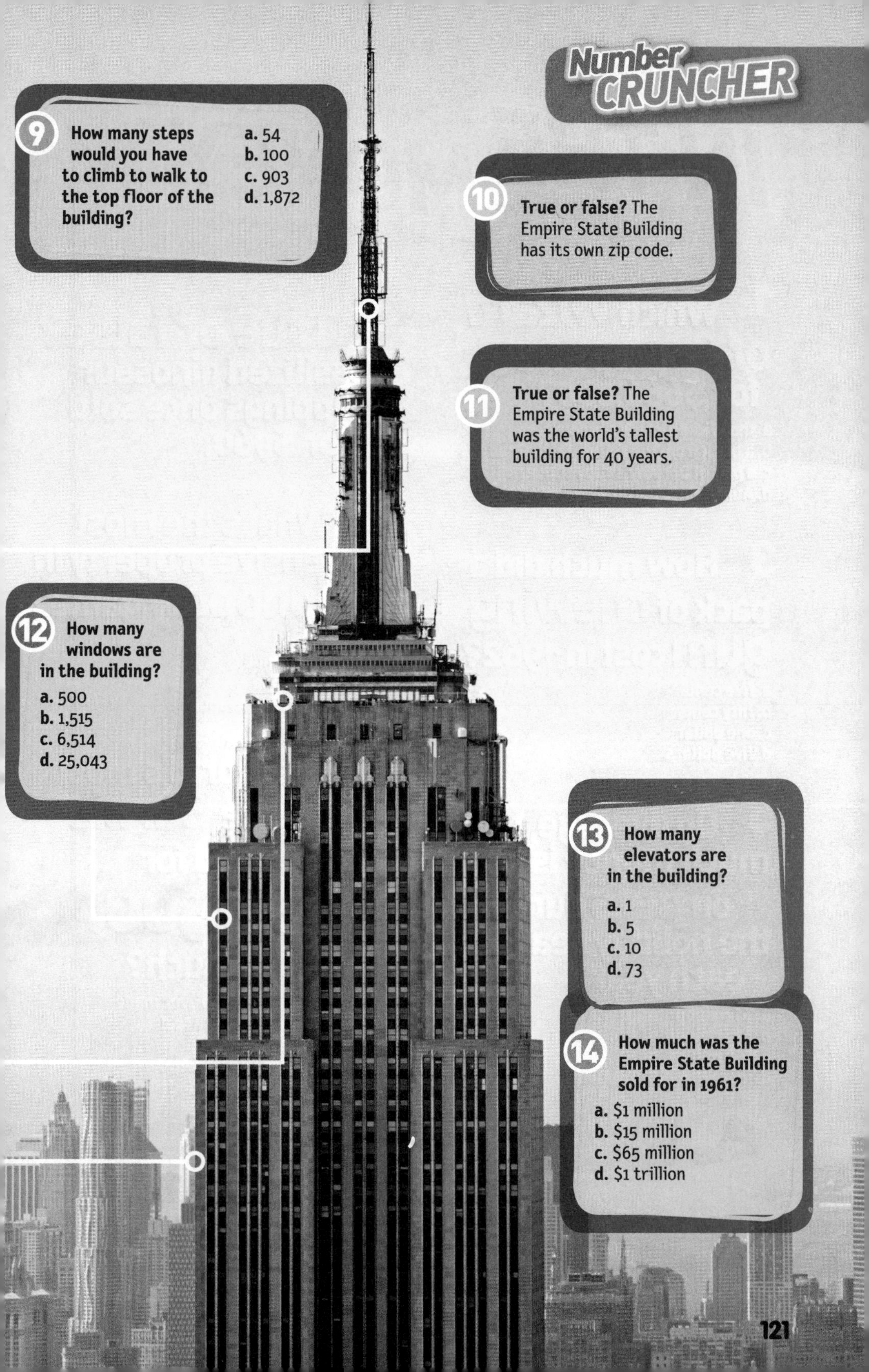

9 **How many steps would you have to climb to walk to the top floor of the building?**

a. 54
b. 100
c. 903
d. 1,872

10 **True or false?** The Empire State Building has its own zip code.

11 **True or false?** The Empire State Building was the world's tallest building for 40 years.

12 **How many windows are in the building?**

a. 500
b. 1,515
c. 6,514
d. 25,043

13 **How many elevators are in the building?**

a. 1
b. 5
c. 10
d. 73

14 **How much was the Empire State Building sold for in 1961?**

a. $1 million
b. $15 million
c. $65 million
d. $1 trillion

IN THE MONEY

1 Which *Wizard of Oz* prop sold for $666,000?

a. the Wicked Witch's broom
b. a brick from the Yellow Brick Road
c. a pair of Dorothy's ruby slippers
d. Auntie Em's apron

2 True or false? Fossilized dinosaur droppings once sold for $960.

3 How much did a pack of chewing gum cost in 1962?

a. five cents
b. fifty cents
c. one dollar
d. five dollars

4 What's the most expensive property in a Monopoly game?

a. Boardwalk
b. Atlantic Avenue
c. Illinois Avenue
d. North Carolina Avenue

5 On average, how much money is spent on pets during the holiday season each year?

a. $1 million
b. $25 million
c. $50 million
d. more than $210 million

6 The world's most expensive Barbie doll sold for $302,500. Why so much?

a. It was the first Barbie ever made.
b. The doll was wearing a real diamond necklace.
c. It came with a toy Corvette.
d. It was the only redheaded Barbie ever made.

7 True or false? The world's most expensive dog collar costs $3.2 million.

8 Which country has more billionaires than anywhere else in the world?

a. India
b. China
c. United States
d. Russia

9 True or false?

The world's most expensive sneakers sold for $1,000.

10 How much did it cost to mail a first-class letter in 1925?

a. two cents
b. ten cents
c. thirty-three cents
d. ten dollars

11 The most expensive tree house, located in England, U.K., has a restaurant inside! How much would you have to pay to have one in your backyard?

a. $100
b. $25,000
c. $100,000
d. $7 million

12 A *Star Wars* fan shelled out $206,000 for which collectible item?

a. an ewok costume
b. a stormtrooper helmet
c. Luke Skywalker's lightsaber
d. the *Millennium Falcon*

13 A line of 84,480 pennies would stretch for a mile. How much money would that add up to?

a. $84.80
b. $844.80
c. $840,000
d. $84 million

14 How much did movie popcorn cost in 1929?

a. five cents
b. fifty cents
c. one dollar
d. ten dollars

CHECK YOUR ANSWERS ON PAGES 132-133.

TRUE or FALSE?

Count It Up!

1. A DOMINO'S EMPLOYEE ONCE TRAVELED 10,532 MILES (16,950 KM) TO DELIVER A PIZZA FROM LONDON, ENGLAND, TO MELBOURNE, AUSTRALIA.
2. THE WORLD'S LARGEST SPORTS STADIUM CAN SEAT 40,000 FANS.
3. THE WORLD'S LONGEST RUNNING TELEVISION SHOW TO DATE HAS BEEN ON THE AIR FOR MORE THAN 65 YEARS.
4. A SUPERSIZED BLT SANDWICH CONTAINED 300 POUNDS (136 KG) OF BACON.
5. THE OLDEST KNOWN PERSON TO DO A BACKFLIP INTO A SWIMMING POOL WAS 45.
6. A 13-YEAR-OLD GIRL SENT 14,528 TEXT MESSAGES IN ONE MONTH.
7. A SCHOOLTEACHER IN ENGLAND PLAYED *DANCE DANCE REVOLUTION* FOR MORE THAN 20 HOURS STRAIGHT.
8. "123456" WAS THE MOST COMMON PASSWORD USED FOR HOTMAIL ACCOUNTS UNTIL 2009.
9. THE WORLD'S LONGEST BRIDGE OVER WATER IS 2 MILES (3.2 KM) LONG.
10. SINGER JUSTIN BIEBER HELD THE RECORD FOR THE MOST TWITTER FOLLOWERS IN 2011.
11. IF YOU STOOD THE WORLD'S LONGEST PENCIL ON END, IT WOULD BE TALLER THAN THE STATUE OF LIBERTY IN NEW YORK, U.S.A.
12. THE TINIEST HORSE ON RECORD WAS ABOUT THE SIZE OF A JACK RUSSELL TERRIER.
13. BAKERS IN ENGLAND, U.K., MADE A 150-POUND (69-KG) CAKE FOR DOGS.
14. THE OLDEST PERSON TO GRADUATE FROM COLLEGE WAS 50 YEARS OLD.
15. A BRITISH ARTIST KNIT AN ACTUAL-SIZE MODEL OF A FERRARI SPORTS CAR.

16 A MINNESOTA RESIDENT HAD AN EMAIL ADDRESS THAT WAS 411 CHARACTERS LONG.

17 AN ICICLE IN SCOTLAND WAS ALMOST AS TALL AS A THREE-STORY BUILDING.

18 IT'S POSSIBLE TO BLOW A CHEWING GUM BUBBLE THAT'S AS BIG AS AN INFLATABLE BEACH BALL.

19 THE LONGEST-PLAYING SONG IS EXPECTED TO TAKE MORE THAN 600 YEARS TO PLAY.

20 A LETTER WAS DELIVERED 73 YEARS AFTER IT WAS MAILED.

21 CHAMPION EATER JOEY CHESTNUT CAN GULP DOWN 200 HOT DOGS IN TEN MINUTES.

22 THE WORLD'S LARGEST JIGSAW PUZZLE HAS 500 PIECES.

23 YOU CAN BUY A GIANT GUMMY BEAR THAT IS 5,000 TIMES LARGER THAN A REGULAR GUMMY BEAR.

24 THERE WAS A MOVIE THAT TOOK TEN DAYS TO WATCH FROM BEGINNING TO END.

25 THE CASPIAN SEA IS THE WORLD'S LARGEST LAKE AT 143,200 SQUARE MILES (371,000 SQ KM).

26 THERE WAS A GIANT ICE-CREAM CONE FILLED WITH ENOUGH OF THE TREAT TO MAKE MORE THAN 600 SINGLE-SCOOP CONES.

27 THE TALLEST DOG BREED IS THE GOLDEN RETRIEVER.

28 FAST-TALKER JOHN MOSCHITTA, JR., CAN SAY 586 WORDS IN ONE MINUTE.

29 THE WORLD'S LARGEST SHOES ARE 17 FEET (5 M) LONG.

30 THERE'S A STREET IN SCOTLAND THAT'S ONLY ABOUT AS LONG AS A BED.

CHECK YOUR ANSWERS ON PAGES 132-133.

Sports STATS

1 **In 2008, this athlete signed the highest paying contract in sports: $275 million over ten years!**

a. baseball player Alex Rodriguez
b. soccer player Cristiano Ronaldo
c. basketball player LeBron James
d. football player Carson Palmer

2 **How many stitches are there in a baseball?**

a. 2
b. 30
c. 50
d. 108

3 **True or false?** Scientists searching for the Loch Ness monster found 100,000 golf balls in the famous Scottish lake, but no monster.

4 **Bowling three strikes in a row is called a _____.**

a. triple strike
b. gutter
c. turkey
d. stinker

5 **One of the world's most famous car races is called the Indy _____.**

a. 100
b. 500
c. 1,000
d. 10,000

6 **What is the world record for most teeth lost during a player's career in the National Hockey League?**

a. 3
b. 7
c. 10
d. 12

A zero in tennis is called ______.

a. loser
b. love
c. deuce
d. doughnut

The Boston Red Sox failed to win Major League Baseball's World Series from 1918 to 2004. What was the name of the curse that some blamed for the 86-year losing streak?

a. The Red Sox Slump
b. The Boston Boogie Monster
c. The Curse of the Bambino
d. The Red Scare

Why did a dinner table designed for basketball legend Michael Jordan have 32,292 holes in it?

a. so he could practice dunking basketballs during dinner
b. so he could practice hitting golf balls during dinner
c. to represent every basket he scored as a pro basketball player
d. none of the above, the table was defective

A referee at the FIFA World Cup runs how many miles during an average game?

a. 3
b. 5
c. 12
d. 30

In what sport would you see a triple lutz?

a. table tennis
b. cheerleading
c. figure skating
d. volleyball

In American football, a team gets six points for what?

a. first down
b. field goal
c. touchdown
d. winning the game

CHECK YOUR ANSWERS ON PAGES 132-133.

MAP MANIA!

GLOBAL DIGITS

Test your knowledge of these nations by the numbers.

1 CHINA

In China, 74 billion ____ are made each year.

a. cars
b. pairs of wooden chopsticks
c. jack-o'-lanterns
d. inline skates

NORTH AMERICA

SOUTH AMERICA

2 SWITZERLAND

True or false? The Swiss eat an average of 25 pounds (11 kg) of chocolate per person each year—more than people in any other country.

PAPUA NEW GUINEA MAN IN CEREMONIAL DRESS

3 PAPUA NEW GUINEA

____ languages are spoken in this country, more than in any other country in the world.

a. 2
b. 12
c. 125
d. 850

SPORTS FANS IN THE NETHERLANDS

4 NETHERLANDS

The Netherlands has the tallest people, on average, of any country in the world. How tall is the average man in this European nation?

a. 4 feet (1.22 m)
b. 5 feet (1.52 m)
c. 6 feet (1.83 m)
d. 10 feet (3.05 m)

B
EUROPE
C
ASIA
E
D
AFRICA
F
AUSTRALIA
ANTARCTICA

PYRAMID IN SUDAN

5 SUDAN

True or false? Sudan has the greatest number of pyramids of any country in the world.

6 WALES, UNITED KINGDOM

True or false? There are more sheep than people in this country.

FLOCK OF SHEARED SHEEP

7-12 EACH OF THESE

COUNTRIES IS HIGHLIGHTED IN ORANGE ON THE MAP. MATCH EACH COUNTRY TO THE CORRECT LOCATION.

CHECK YOUR ANSWERS ON PAGES 132-133.

GAME SHOW

ULTIMATE NUMBER CHALLENGE

1 How many peanuts does it take to make a 12-ounce (340-g) jar of peanut butter?

a. 5
b. 540
c. 1,400
d. 5 million

2

TRUE OR FALSE?

One of George Washington's library books was 221 years overdue.

3 How many bones are in your elbow?

a. 0
b. 1
c. 3
d. 8

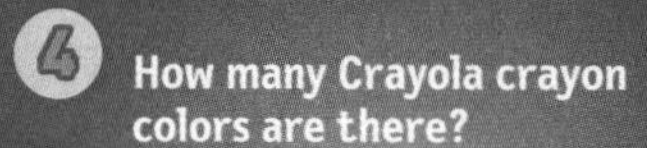

4 How many Crayola crayon colors are there?

a. 20
b. 55
c. 120
d. 500

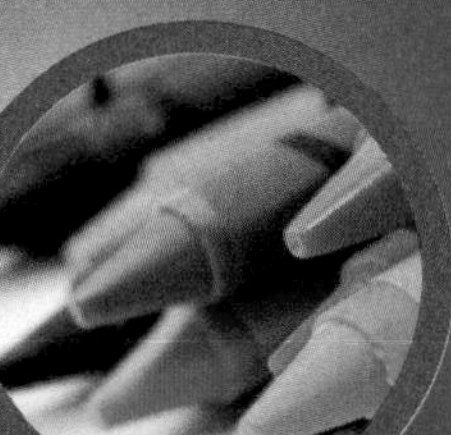

5 How many dimples are there in a golf ball?

a. 1
b. 25
c. at least 50
d. at least 250

6 How long does it take an unopened bag of marshmallows to expire?

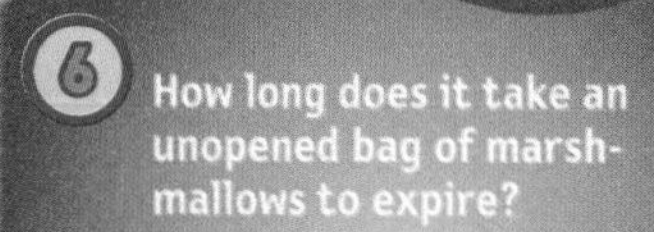

a. one day
b. one week
c. ten months
d. ten years

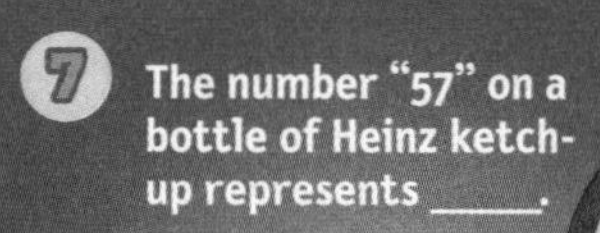

7 The number "57" on a bottle of Heinz ketchup represents ______.

a. the number of tomatoes used to make the ketchup in the bottle

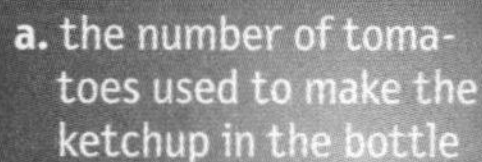

b. the number of different kinds of pickles the company once sold
c. 57 cents, the original price of the ketchup
d. 1957, the year the ketchup was invented

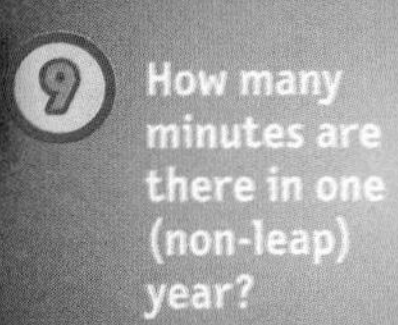

8 How many Popsicle sticks were used to make this actual-size re-creation of a Viking boat?

a. 5,000
b. 15 million
c. 100 million
d. 5 billion

9 How many minutes are there in one (non-leap) year?

a. 60
b. 365
c. 525,600
d. 1 trillion

10 Triskaidekaphobia is the fear of ______.

a. five-headed monsters
b. the number 13
c. two-door sports cars
d. triplets

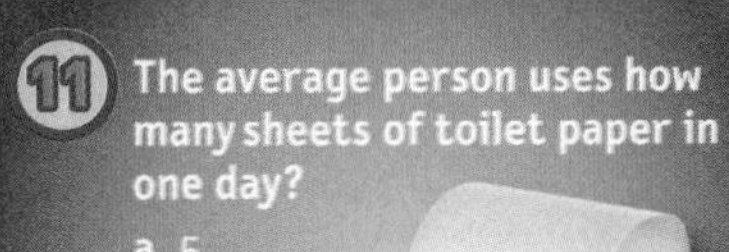

11 The average person uses how many sheets of toilet paper in one day?

a. 5
b. 27
c. 57
d. 100

12 TRUE OR FALSE?

There are 32 million bacteria on each square inch of your skin.

13 In what year was the first macaroni-and-cheese recipe printed?

a. 1824
b. 1975
c. 2002
d. 2011

14 ULTIMATE BRAIN BUSTER

WHICH OF THESE FAMOUS CHARACTERS IS SUPPOSEDLY 542 YEARS OLD?

a. 
Papa Smurf

b. 
Squidward

c. 
The Lorax

d. Puss in Boots

CHECK YOUR ANSWERS ON PAGES 132-133.

ANSWERS

Animal Figures, pages 118-119

1. c
2. d
3. d
4. b
5. b
6. b
7. c
8. b
9. **True**. The African gray parrot, who died in 2007, was famous for his intelligence and language skills.
10. b
11. d
12. d

How the Empire State Building Stacks Up, pages 120-121

1. b
2. c
3. b
4. a
5. a
6. d
7. **True.** On a clear day, you can see five different U.S. states from the top of the skyscraper.
8. c
9. d
10. **True.** The Empire State Building's zip code is 10118.
11. **True.** The building was the world's tallest until 1972.
12. c
13. d
14. c

In the Money, pages 122-123

1. c
2. **True.** The 130-million-year-old fossil was bought by a man in Ohio, U.S.A.
3. a
4. a
5. d
6. b
7. **True.** The "Amour, Amour" dog collar is made with 1,600 diamonds.
8. c
9. **False.** The gold-dipped sneakers sold for $4,053!
10. a
11. d
12. c
13. b
14. a

True or False? Count It Up! pages 124-125

1. **True.** This special delivery was done to raise money for a charity.
2. **False.** North Korea's May Day stadium can seat 150,000 fans.
3. **True.** The news program *Meet the Press* first aired in 1947.
4. **True.** The sandwich, created during a tomato festival in Bradley, Arkansas, U.S.A., also contained 60 pounds (27 kg) of tomatoes and about 80 pounds (36 grams) of lettuce.
5. **False.** Walter Liesner of Germany did a backflip into a swimming pool when he was 94.
6. **True.** Fortunately, the girl had an unlimited text messaging plan.
7. **True.** Chris McGivern played the game for 20 hours, 24 minutes, and 43 seconds.
8. **True.** Out of 10,000 emails sampled by a security expert, 123456 was used 64 times.
9. **False.** The Jiaozhou Bay Bridge in China is 26.3 miles (42.3 km) long.
10. **False.** With more than 11 million followers, pop star Lady Gaga held the record.
11. **True.** The pencil, created by a writing-supplies company in Germany, measured 738 feet, 10 inches (225.21 m). The Statue of Liberty is 305 feet, 1 inch (93 m) tall.
12. **True.** A pinto stallion named Einstein stood 14 inches (36 cm) tall.
13. **True.** The cake was made in honor of the royal wedding of Prince William and Kate Middleton in 2011.
14. **False.** An Oregon man graduated from college when he was 99 years old.
15. **True.** She used 12 miles (19 km) of yarn to knit the sports car.
16. **True.** His email address was: hi-this-is-the-longest-email-in-the-world-and-is-much-superior-to-contact-admin-hello-webmaster-info-services-peter-crazy-but-oh-so-ubber-cool-english-alphabet-loverer-abcdef ghijklmnopqrstuvwxyz-at-please-try-to. send-me-an-email-if-you-can-pos sibly-begin-to-remember-this-coz. this-is-the-longest-email-address-known-to-man-but-to-be-honest.this-is-such-a-stupidly-long-sub-domain-it-could-go-on-forever@zchr.org. The email address is no longer active.
17. **True.** An icicle that measured 27 feet (8 m) hung from a bridge in Scotland—that's almost three stories tall.
18. **True.** An Alabama man blew a bubble that was 20 inches (50.8 cm) wide, about the size of a beach ball.
19. **True.** A self-playing organ in Germany began playing the song in 2000 and is expected to finish in the year 2639.
20. **True.** The letter was postmarked on December 23, 1937, in San Francisco, California, U.S.A. It arrived in Stockton, California, U.S.A., in 2010.
21. **False.** Chestnut ate 68 hot dogs in 10 minutes.
22. **False.** A 551,232-piece puzzle with a picture of a lotus flower was created by students in Vietnam.
23. **True.** There's a website that sells 27-pound (12-kg) gummy bears that are almost a foot and a half (43 cm) tall.
24. **True.** A group of Danish artists showed a film that ran for 240 hours straight—that's 24 hours a day for ten days!
25. **True.** Even though it's called a sea, the Caspian is considered a lake.
26. **True.** Italian candymakers created the nine-foot-tall cone (2.7 m) during the International Exhibition of Ice Cream in 2011.
27. **False.** The world's tallest dog breed is the Irish Wolfhound, which is about 34 inches (86 cm) tall at the shoulder.
28. **True.** Moschitta has appeared in hundreds of commercials and television shows.
29. **True.** You'd have to be 125 feet tall (3,810 cm) in order for the shoes to fit.
30. **True.** A street called Ebenezer Place, in Caithness, Scotland, is only 6.9 feet (2.05 m) long! A typical twin bed is about 6.25 feet (1.9 m) long.

Sports Stats, pages 126-127

1. **a**
2. **d**
3. **True.** A research team called SeaTrepid found the balls. They believe people once practiced their golf swings by hitting balls into the lake.
4. **c**
5. **b**
6. **d**
7. **b**
8. **c**
9. **c**
10. **c**
11. **c**
12. **c**

Map Mania! Global Digits, pages 128-129

1. **b**
2. **True.** That's equal to about 284 regular Hershey's bars per person each year.
3. **d**
4. **c**
5. **True.** Sudan has 220 pyramids, more than any other country. Egypt has 138.
6. **True.** There are about 11 million sheep and some 3 million people in Wales.
7. **China - E**
8. **Switzerland - C**
9. **Papua New Guinea - F**
10. **Netherlands - B**
11. **Sudan - D**
12. **Wales, U.K. - A**

Game Show: Ultimate Number Challenge, pages 130-131

1. **b**
2. **True.** Washington borrowed the book from a library in New York, U.S.A., in 1789. It was returned in 2010. If Washington were around today, he would be charged $300,000 for his overdue book!
3. **c**
4. **c**
5. **d**
6. **c**
7. **b**
8. **b**
9. **c**
10. **b**
11. **c**
12. **True.** Don't worry! Most of the bacteria on your skin are harmless.
13. **a**
14. **a**

SCORING

0-36

WHO'S COUNTING?

Mind-numbing numbers may not be your thing. You'd probably rather read a novel than do fractions any day. You can't get out of math class, but you can figure out what you love to do, and learn to do it really well.

37-73

IT ALL ADDS UP

You've got tons of numbers swimming around in your noggin. A champ at trivia games, you probably impress your friends and family with how much you know.

74-109

MATHE-*MAGICIAN!*

You're practically a human calculator! You love random trivia and have never met a fact or figure that you couldn't memorize. You could grow up to be an astronaut, or a physicist, or the next Einstein!

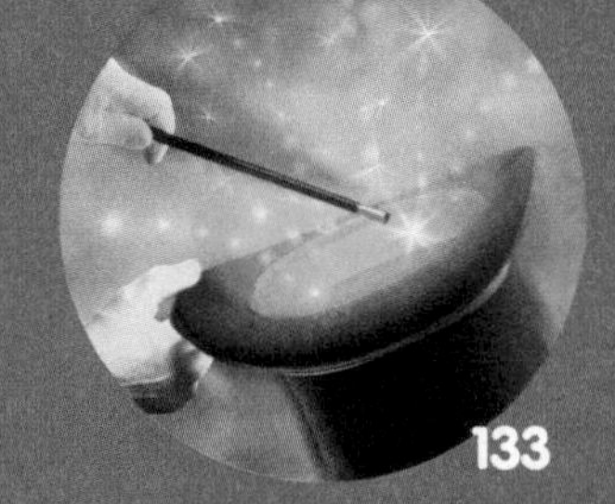

TAKE ME TO YOUR LEADER.

It's Not Rocket SCIENCE

DUDE, I AM YOUR LEADER.

THE HUMAN BODY

1 **About how many hairs do most people lose every day?**

a. 10 strands
b. 35 strands
c. 50 strands
d. 75 strands

2 **The cerebellum is a part of your brain located at the back of the head. Without it you wouldn't be able to ____.**

a. remember your homework
b. blink your eyes
c. kick a soccer ball
d. breathe

3 **The most common eye color in the world is ____.**

a. brown
b. blue
c. green
d. hazel

4 **How fast does air rush out of your nose when you sneeze?**

a. up to 10 miles an hour (16 kph)
b. up to 25 miles an hour (40 kph)
c. up to 50 miles an hour (80 kph)
d. up to 100 miles an hour (161 kph)

5 **True or false?** Your sense of smell is the strongest in the morning.

6 **How many muscles do you use when you talk?**

a. 45
b. 55
c. 72
d. 87

7 **How many breaths does the average person take each day?**

a. 50
b. 150
c. 5,000
d. 25,000

8 **What does mucus do?**

a. filters out harmful bacteria
b. helps you smell
c. helps your lungs take in oxygen
d. stops your nose from collapsing

9 **Your heart is the size of ____.**

a. a marble
b. a walnut
c. your fist
d. a watermelon

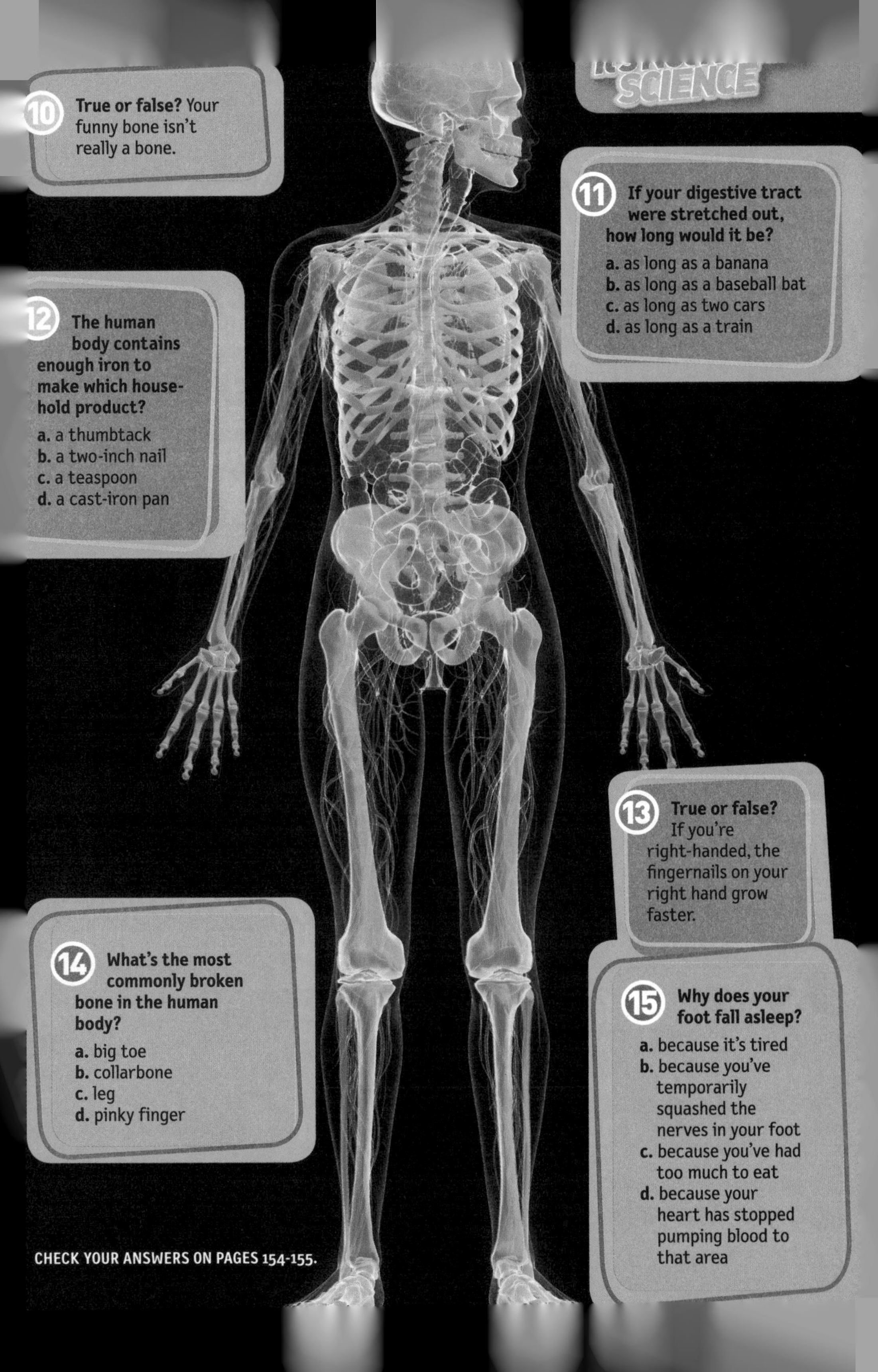

CHECK YOUR ANSWERS ON PAGES 154-155.

INCREDIBLE INVENTIONS

1 Which classic amusement park ride was modeled after a bicycle wheel?

a. bumper car
b. Ferris wheel
c. roller coaster
d. tea cup ride

2 True or false? The Popsicle was invented by an 11-year-old boy.

3 True or false? A man invented a ringtone that can be heard only by young people.

4 Most experts believe fireworks were invented in what country?

a. Greece
b. Egypt
c. Canada
d. China

5 Before modern toothbrushes were invented in 1938, what were toothbrush bristles made of?

a. horsehair
b. porcupine quills
c. cat whiskers
d. hog hair

6 In 1782, Joseph Michel Montgolfier filled a silk bag with hot air. What did he invent?

a. a birthday balloon
b. an air mattress
c. a hot-air balloon
d. water wings

7 The first cell phone weighed two pounds (0.9 kg), the weight of ____ iPhones.

a. three
b. four
c. five
d. six

8 In the movie *Hugo*, what invention does Hugo try to repair?

a. a camera
b. an automaton
c. a radio
d. a video game console

9 In the movie *The Nutty Professor* Sherman Klump invents a special potion. What does it do?

a. makes his hair fall out
b. makes him skinny
c. makes him grow
d. makes him fly

10 Before the invention of penicillin, what was often used to clean infected wounds?

a. soup
b. worms
c. aspirin
d. maggots

11 The "Snurfer"—a flat board that people used to "surf" on snow—led to what invention?

a. surfboard
b. skateboard
c. snowboard
d. kiteboard

12 TOPIO is a humanoid robot that is designed to ___.

a. clean your room
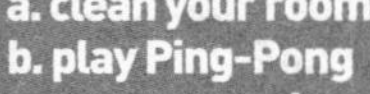
b. play Ping-Pong
c. rescue people
d. explore planets

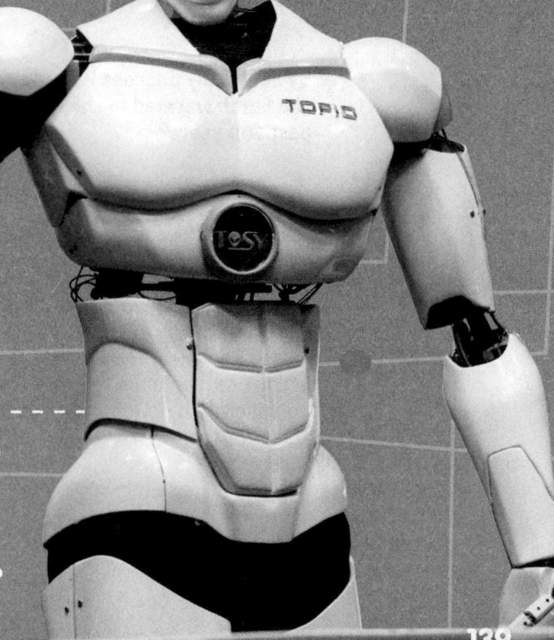

13 True or false? The fortune cookie was invented in China.

CHECK YOUR ANSWERS ON PAGES 154-155.

ECO-QUIZ

1 **Which of these items can be composted?**

a. eggshells
b. golf balls
c. aluminum foil
d. all of the above

2 **Which of the following is the biggest energy guzzler?**

a. clothes dryer
b. refrigerator
c. iron
d. hair dryer

3 **In your lifetime, you will throw away enough trash to fill ___.**

a. the Empire State Building
b. about five garbage trucks
c. six bathtubs
d. the Grand Canyon

4 **In the futuristic movie *Wall-E*, the little robot the movie is named for has a special job. What is it?**

a. cleaning up trash left behind by humans
b. planting trees in parks
c. designing eco-friendly tourist destinations
d. sorting bottles at a recycling plant

5 **By how many degrees has the Earth warmed in the past 100 years?**

a. 1°F (0.6°C)
b. 12°F (7°C)
c. 20°F (11°C)
d. 30°F (17°C)

6 **Which statement about recycling is true?**

a. More than half of all aluminum cans produced in the United States are recycled.
b. Roughly 100,000 aluminum cans are recycled every minute in the United States.
c. Recycling one aluminum can saves nearly enough energy to power a 100-watt lightbulb for four hours.
d. all of the above

7. **What is the most frequently found trash in beach cleanups?**
   - **a.** glass
   - **b.** pieces of plastic
   - **c.** shoes
   - **d.** jewelry

8. **Paper can be made from which of these materials?**
   - **a.** panda droppings
   - **b.** hemp
   - **c.** wood
   - **d.** all of the above

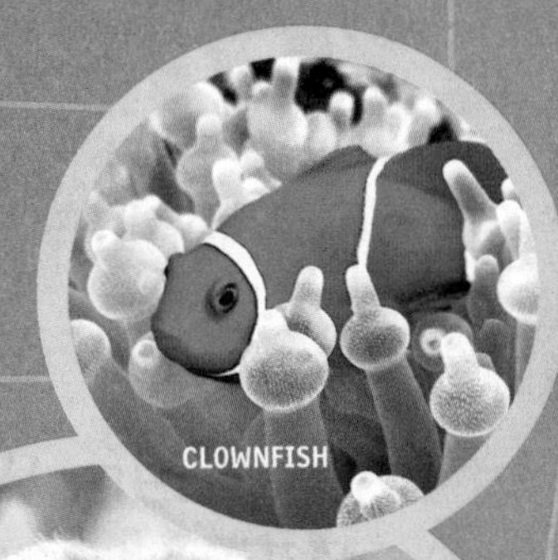

9. **Which of the following uses the least amount of energy?**
   - **a.** stove
   - **b.** toaster over
   - **c.** microwave
   - **d.** refrigerator

10. **Which of the following animals are threatened by global warming?**
    - **a.** polar bears
    - **b.** clownfish
    - **c.** koalas
    - **d.** all of the above

KOALA

11. **What should you have on your bed when it gets chilly?**
    - **a.** an electric blanket
    - **b.** only a bedsheet
    - **c.** no blankets, just crank up the heat
    - **d.** lots of blankets

12. **After baby leatherback sea turtles hatch on beaches, they head straight for the sea. Which of these is a big threat to them along the way?**
    - **a.** City lights disorient the turtles.
    - **b.** Sand castles are like mountains in their paths.
    - **c.** Water rafts can trap them.
    - **d.** They can mistake beach balls for their mothers.

CHECK YOUR ANSWERS ON PAGES 154-155.

VOLCANIC BLAST!

1 Where would you find **Olympus Mons**—the largest volcano in the solar system?

a. Earth
b. Mars
c. Saturn
d. the moon

2 About how many **active volcanoes** exist on Earth?

a. 100 b. 600 c. 1,900 d. 10,000

3 What color is lava at its **hottest**?

a. yellow
b. magenta
c. red
d. blue

4 What is the name of the **belt of volcanoes** that encircles the rim of the **Pacific Ocean**?

a. Ring of Fire
b. Hoop of Heat
c. Loop of Lava
d. Circle of Death

5 The eruption of an Iceland volcano in 2010 caused a **major problem.** What was it?

a. It grounded flights in Europe.
b. It melted polar glaciers.
c. It buried Iceland's capital city in ash.
d. It destroyed Iceland.

6 What type of rock is formed by volcanic activity?

a. sedimentary
b. igneous
c. limestone
d. Pop Rocks

7 Which famous volcano buried Pompeii in A.D. 79?

a. Mount Kilimanjaro
b. Mount Vesuvius
c. Mount St. Helens
d. Mount Etna

8 True or false? There are underwater volcanoes.

9 Where does the word "volcano" come from?

a. volume
b. *Star Trek*
c. the ancient Roman god Vulcan
d. the Italian word for "angry"

10 Which of the following is not a type of volcano?

a. shield
b. composite
c. blaster
d. cinder cone

11 How much of Earth's surface has been created by volcanoes?

a. 0 percent
b. 50 percent
c. less than 40 percent
d. more than 80 percent

12 How hot can lava get?

a. up to 250°F (121°C)
b. more than 1000°F (538°C)
c. more than 2000°F (1093°C)
d. up to 10,000°F (5538°C)

13 What is the tallest volcano on Earth?

a. Mauna Kea, Hawaii, U.S.A.
b. Krakatoa, Indonesia
c. Mount Fuji, Honshu, Japan
d. El Chichón, Chiapas, Mexico

CHECK YOUR ANSWERS ON PAGES 154-155.

TRUE or FALSE?

SPACED OUT

1 HALLEY'S COMET IS THE NAME OF THE FAMOUS COMET THAT ZIPS PAST EARTH EVERY 75 TO 76 YEARS.

2 ASTRONAUTS WHO RETURNED TO EARTH FROM EARLY MOON MISSIONS WERE QUARANTINED.

3 A STAR AT THE END OF ITS LIFE CYCLE IS CALLED A WHITE DWARF.

4 A BULLFROG ONCE TRAVELED INTO SPACE.

5 A TEN-YEAR-OLD KID ON EARTH WOULD BE 42 YEARS OLD ON MERCURY.

6 THE CONSTELLATION URSA MAJOR FORMS THE IMAGE OF A UNICORN.

7 A GIANT STORM ON JUPITER, CALLED THE GREAT RED SPOT, IS ABOUT AS WIDE AS EARTH.

8 SATURN IS THE ONLY PLANET IN THE SOLAR SYSTEM THAT HAS RINGS.

9 CHARLIE BROWN WAS THE NAME OF A COMMAND MODULE ON A NASA MISSION TO THE MOON.

10 SIRIUS IS OFTEN CALLED THE "DOG STAR," BECAUSE IT'S PART OF CANIS MAJOR, A CONSTELLATION THAT LOOKS LIKE A LARGE DOG.

11 MERCURY IS THE SMALLEST PLANET IN THE SOLAR SYSTEM.

12 IN THE MOVIE *TOY STORY*, THE FAMOUS SPACE RANGER IS NAMED EMPEROR ZURG.

13 ASTRONAUTS HAVE GROWN PEAS ON THE SPACE SHUTTLE.

14 ASTRONAUT ALAN SHEPARD PLAYED GOLF ON THE MOON.

15 MOST COMETS HAVE ONE TAIL.

16 THE WORLD'S HIGHEST OBSERVATORY—A BUILDING FROM WHICH SCIENTISTS VIEW SPACE OBJECTS—SITS ON A VOLCANO IN CHILE.

17 THE MOON CREATES LIGHT.

18 MEAT LOAF WAS THE FIRST FOOD ASTRONAUTS ATE IN SPACE.

19 THE PLANET TATOOINE IN THE *STAR WARS* MOVIES IS BASED ON A REAL-LIFE DWARF PLANET CALLED TATTOO.

20 MARS, SOMETIMES CALLED THE "RED PLANET," GETS ITS COLOR FROM RUST IN ITS SOIL.

21 ONE DAY ON THE MOON LASTS 27 EARTH DAYS.

22 THE AVERAGE TEMPERATURE OF THE SUN'S SURFACE IS A SIZZLING 10,000°F (5500°C).

23 THE LONGEST SPACE WALK EVER LASTED 8 HOURS AND 56 MINUTES.

24 THE BILLIONS OF STARS IN THE MILKY WAY FORM A CONE SHAPE.

25 IF YOU WEIGH 100 POUNDS (45 KG) ON EARTH, YOU WOULD WEIGH 38 POUNDS (17 KG) ON MARS.

26 IT WOULD TAKE ABOUT 20 YEARS FOR A SPACECRAFT TO TRAVEL FROM EARTH TO PLUTO.

27 ASTRONAUTS "GROW" IN SPACE.

28 ALL ASTEROIDS ARE MADE OF FIRE.

29 THE CRATERS ON THE MOON WERE CAUSED BY SPACE SHUTTLE LANDINGS.

30 IN RUSSIA, "ASTRONAUTS" ARE CALLED COSMONAUTS.

CHECK YOUR ANSWERS ON PAGES 154-155.

WEATHER!

1 Which of the following was a hurricane name?

a. Mickey Mouse
b. Katrina
c. The Terminator
d. Windy Wilma

2 In 2004, a powerful earthquake in the Indian Ocean triggered a deadly ___, which flooded many countries.

a. landslide
b. tsunami
c. hurricane
d. sandstorm

3 How fast can lightning travel?

a. 70 miles an hour (113 kph)
b. 1,300 miles an hour (2,092 kph)
c. 70,000 miles an hour (112,654 kph)
d. 130,000 miles an hour (209,215 kph)

4 The largest hailstone measured wider than a ___.

a. golf ball
b. tennis ball
c. softball
d. bowling ball

5 The coldest recorded temperature on Earth was -128.6°F (-89.2°C). Where did it take place?

a. Vancouver, Canada
b. Oslo, Norway
c. Vostok Station, Antarctica
d. Hawaii, U.S.A.

6 What is the nickname for the area of the United States that has the most tornadoes on Earth?

a. Tornado Freeway
b. Whirlwind Lane
c. Tornado Alley
d. Spin City

7 In the 1930s, powerful winds created **huge clouds of dirt** in the Great Plains of the United States. This area became known as the ____.

a. Dust Bowl
b. Sand Box
c. Wind Tunnel
d. Beach Town

8 A **hurricane** in the western Pacific Ocean is called what?

a. monsoon
b. thunderstorm
c. typhoon
d. tornado

9 **True or false?** Lightning never strikes the same place twice.

10 A column of **rotating wind** that forms over water is called a ____.

a. torn-sea-ado
b. waterspout
c. waterburp
d. whirlado

11 **True or false?** Humans are responsible for 90 percent of all wildfires.

12 The most dangerous **threat** to people **during a tornado** is ____.

a. loud noises
b. giant hailstones
c. flying objects
d. heavy rain

CHECK YOUR ANSWERS ON PAGES 154-155.

Earth ROCKS!

DIAGRAM OF EARTH'S LAYERS

1. **What is the outermost layer of the Earth called?**
   a. mantle
   b. crust
   c. outer core
   d. magma

2. **___ is the hardest substance on Earth.**
   a. pearl
   b. chalk
   c. molten rock
   d. diamond

3. **Bryce Canyon National Park in Utah, U.S.A., is famous for which type of strange rock formations?**
   a. hoodoos
   b. half domes
   c. mesas
   d. quartz

BRYCE CANYON NATIONAL PARK

4. **What are deep, narrow valleys carved out by erosion called?**
   a. canyons
   b. cliffs
   c. rivers
   d. prairies

5. **What gem is the birth-stone for July and is a symbol of contentment?**
   a. ruby
   b. pearl
   c. amethyst
   d. emerald

6 **True or false?** More meteorites, or space rocks, have been found in Antarctica than any other place on Earth.

7 **What is the name of the iceberg-packed area off the coast of Newfoundland, Canada, where the *Titanic* sank?**

a. Bermuda Triangle
b. Shipwreck Circle
c. Baffin Bay
d. Iceberg Alley

8 **How much of Earth's fresh water is stored in glaciers?**

a. one-quarter
b. half
c. nearly three-quarters
d. almost all fresh water

9 **True or false?** An ice jam once caused Niagara Falls—on the border of New York State, U.S.A., and Ontario, Canada—to stop flowing.

10 **What is the name of the longest cave system in the world, with more than 390 miles (628 km) of mapped passageways?**

a. Blue Grotto, Italy
b. Carlsbad Caverns, United States
c. Lascaux Cave, France
d. Mammoth Cave, United States

11 **Which light blue gemstone is popular in some Native American jewelry?**

a. sapphire
b. turquoise
c. emerald
d. topaz

NIAGARA FALLS

CHECK YOUR ANSWERS ON PAGES 154-155.

Extreme MACHINES

1 **How fast is the world's fastest car?**

a. as fast as a cruise ship
b. as fast as a high-speed train
c. as fast as a jet airplane
d. as fast as a space shuttle

2 **What form of transportation does *not* appear in the *Harry Potter* book series?**

a. a broomstick
b. a hippogriff
c. a skateboard with wings
d. a flying motorcycle

3 **The Maglev train in Japan relies on what to hover above the tracks as it travels?**

a. magnets
b. batteries
c. steam
d. magic

4 **What type of transportation did daredevil Yves Rossy use to fly above the Grand Canyon for eight minutes?**

a. a jet pack
b. a hot-air balloon
c. a helicopter
d. he was shot out of a cannon

5 **Explorer Fabien Cousteau used what kind of vehicle to get an up close view of sharks?**

a. high-tech dive cage
b. sea rover
c. shark-shaped submersible
d. glass-bottom boat

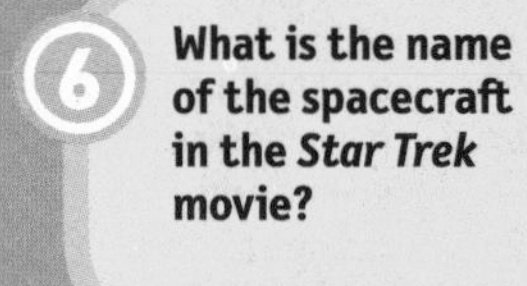

6 **What is the name of the spacecraft in the *Star Trek* movie?**

a. *U.S.S. Enterprise*
b. *Millennium Falcon*
c. *Jupiter 2*
d. *Death Star*

7 ***Bigfoot 5* is the world's biggest monster truck. Each of its tires is about as wide as which of these items?**

a. school desk
b. bicycle
c. small car
d. school bus

8 **True or false?** There's a car that drives on land and in water.

9 **True or false?** There's a scooter that hovers four inches (10 cm) above the ground as you ride it.

SR-71 BLACKBIRD

10 **The *SR-71 Blackbird*—one of the world's fastest aircraft—flew from New York, U.S.A., to London, England, in how long?**

a. a half hour
b. 1 hour and 54 minutes
c. 2 hours and 12 minutes
d. 3 hours

11 **The last space shuttle was retired in 2011. What was the average speed of these spacecrafts when they orbited Earth?**

a. 60 miles an hour (97 kph)
b. 500 miles an hour (805 kph)
c. 1,000 miles an hour (1,609 kph)
d. 17,500 miles an hour (28,164 kph)

12 **Soon tourists will be able to blast off into space aboard a *Virgin Galactic* spacecraft. How much will one round-trip ticket cost?**

a. $5,000
b. $25,000
c. $75,000
d. $200,000

SPACE SHUTTLE

CHECK YOUR ANSWERS ON PAGES 154-155.

GAME SHOW

ULTIMATE SCIENCE CHALLENGE

1

What do you call a person who studies trees?

a. dendrologist
b. paleontologist
c. treeologist
d. geologist

2

The ______ may be the world's stinkiest flower. It smells like rotting flesh!

a. daffodil
b. corpse flower
c. anemone flower
d. English rose

3

TRUE OR FALSE?

The largest bacteria are about the size of the period at the end of this sentence

4

During RoboCup, robots from around the world compete with each other in which sport?

a. baseball
b. running
c. soccer
d. car racing

5

What precious metal is an Olympic gold medal mostly made of?

a. gold
b. silver
c. bronze
d. aluminum

6

The constellation called Ursa Minor contains a famous star pattern, shown below. What is the name of the pattern?

a. The Belt of Orion
b. The Teacup
c. The Northern Cross
d. The Little Dipper

7

TRUE OR FALSE?

The world's largest snowflake was wider than this book.

Thomas Edison is best known for inventing the ______.

a. radio
b. incandescent lightbulb
c. Internet
d. microwave oven

9 **This famous cave, located beneath Mexico's Chihuahuan Desert, is filled with what?**

a. giant icicles
b. chalk pillars
c. giant crystals
d. diamonds

What type of carnivorous plant is this?

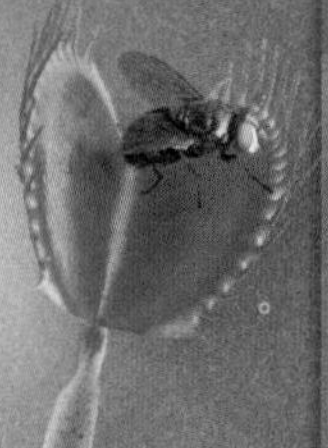

a. pitcher plant
b. Venus flytrap
c. sundew
d. butterwort

What is geliophobia the fear of?

a. jelly
b. puzzles
c. floods
d. laughter

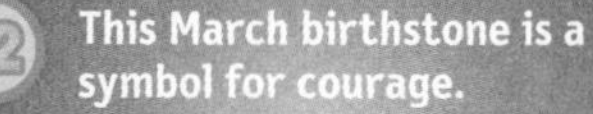

This March birthstone is a symbol for courage.

a. amethyst
b. pearl
c. aquamarine
d. garnet

TRUE OR FALSE?

A peanut is a type of nut.

14 **ULTIMATE BRAIN BUSTER**

Which of these objects contains a green coloring called chlorophyll?

a.
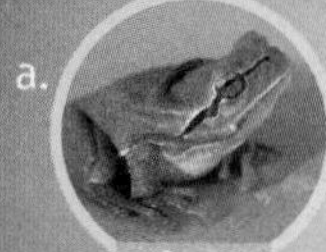

frog

b.

leaf

c.

St. Patrick's Day hat

d.

emerald

CHECK YOUR ANSWERS ON PAGES 154-155.

ANSWERS

Human Body, pages 136-137

1. **d**
2. **c**
3. **a**
4. **d**
5. **False.** Studies show that the human sense of smell is strongest in the evening, but no one is sure why.
6. **c**
7. **d**
8. **a**
9. **c**
10. **True.** Your "funny bone" is really a nerve. It gets its name from the tingling feeling you get in your elbow after you bump it.
11. **c**
12. **b**
13. **True.** Studies have shown that fingernails on your dominant hand grow faster. Using your hand more may increases blood flow to the area, which in turn may stimulate nail growth.
14. **b**
15. **b**

Incredible Inventions, pages 138-139

1. **b**
2. **True.** In 1905, 11-year-old Frank Epperson left a cup on his porch that was filled with powdered soda, water, and a stirring stick. It froze overnight. The next morning, Frank had discovered what would later become known as the Popsicle.
3. **True.** The ringtone, called "The Mosquito," is set at a higher frequency that only people under 25 years old can hear.
4. **d**
5. **d**
6. **c**
7. **d**
8. **b**
9. **b**
10. **d**
11. **c**
12. **b**
13. **False.** The fortune cookie was most likely invented in Japan and brought to the United States by immigrants.

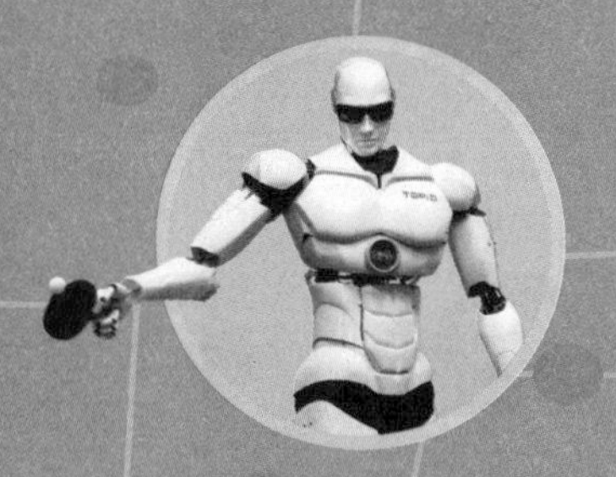

Eco-Quiz, pages 140-141

1. **a**
2. **b**
3. **b**
4. **a**
5. **a***
6. **d**
7. **b**
8. **d**
9. **c**
10. **d**
11. **d**
12. **a**

**When converting to Celsius for temperature change, remember that a change of 32 degrees Fahrenheit equals a change of 17.7 degrees Celsius.*

Volcanic Blast! pages 142-143

1. **b**
2. **c**
3. **d**
4. **a**
5. **a**
6. **b**
7. **b**
8. **True.** Scientists believe that 80 percent of all volcanic eruptions take place underwater.
9. **c**
10. **c**
11. **d**
12. **c**
13. **a**

True or False? Spaced Out! pages 144-145

1. **True.** Halley's Comet was last visible in 1986.
2. **True.** Astronauts were quarantined to prevent the spread of moon germs. Today, scientists know that there is no such thing as moon germs.
3. **True.** White dwarf stars are believed to be the final evolutionary cycle of small stars.
4. **True.** Many animals have traveled into space on spaceships, including a bullfrog, a dog, and a chimpanzee.
5. **True.** Your age is the number of years you have lived. Since one year on Mercury is equal to about 88 Earth days, you'd have lived more years on Mercury.
6. **False.** Ursa Major is shaped like a giant bear.
7. **True.** Earth's diameter at the Equator is 7,926 miles (12,756 km). The Great Red Spot is from 7,456 miles to 8,699 miles wide (12,000–14,000 km).
8. **False.** Jupiter, Uranus, and Neptune also have rings.
9. **True.** *Charlie Brown* was the name of the command module that orbited the moon on NASA's Apollo 10 mission, in May 1969. The lunar module, which flew within 50,000 feet (15,240 m) of the moon's surface, was named Snoopy.
10. **True.** Sirius is the brightest star in Canis Major and the brightest star visible from Earth.
11. **True.** Mercury became the smallest planet in 2006 when Pluto's status was changed to a "dwarf planet."
12. **False.** Buzz Lightyear is the fictional space ranger. Emperor Zurg is his enemy.
13. **True.** Astronauts have also grown other foods in space, such as potatoes and radishes.
14. **True.** Shepard used a makeshift golf club to hit two golf balls on the moon in 1971, during the Apollo 14 mission.
15. **False.** Most comets have two tails: one made from dust and the other from gas.
16. **True.** The University of Tokyo Atacama Observatory (TAO) sits on top of Chile's Cerro Chajnantor volcano, at an altitude of 18,500 feet (5,639 m).
17. **False:** The reflection of the sun's light on the moon causes the moon to shine.
18. **False.** Astronaut John Glenn became the first person to eat in space when he ate applesauce from a tube aboard the Friendship 7 in 1961.
19. **False.** The planet Tatooine is completely made-up.
20. **True.** Mars gets its color from a chemical compound called iron oxide, which is also known as rust.
21. **True.** It takes the moon 27 Earth days to complete a rotation on its axis.
22. **True.** The sun's core is even hotter: 26,999,540°F (14,999,727°C)!
23. **True.** NASA astronauts Susan Helms and John Voss performed the spacewalk in 2001 to do maintenance work on the International Space Station.
24. **False.** The stars of the Milky Way form a spiral shape.
25. **True.** Because the pull of gravity on Mars is less than on Earth, you would weigh less on Mars.
26. **False.** The flight takes about nine years. NASA launched a spacecraft called New Horizon in 2006 that is expected to fly by Pluto in 2015.
27. **True.** Because there is less gravity in space than there is on Earth, an astronaut's spine can stretch by about one to two inches.
28. **False.** Asteroids are made of rocks and metals.
29. **False.** The moon's craters were caused by collisions with asteroids, comets, and other space objects.
30. **True.** The word comes from the Greek words *kosmos*, which means universe, and *nautes*, which means sailor.

Wild Weather! pages 146-147

1. **b**
2. **b**
3. **d**
4. **d**
5. **c**
6. **c**
7. **a**
8. **c**
9. **False.** Although it is rare, it is possible for lightning to strike the same place twice.
10. **b**
11. **True**. While there are many ways humans start wildfires, campfires left burning are one of the common causes.
12. **c**

Earth Rocks! pages 148-149

1. **b**
2. **d**
3. **a**
4. **a**
5. **a**
6. **True.** The space rocks in Antarctica are preserved in ice and easy to spot.
7. **d**
8. **c**
9. **True.** On March 29, 1948, an ice jam in the upper river caused Niagara Falls to stop flowing for several hours.
10. **d**
11. **b**

Extreme Machines, pages 150-151

1. **c**
2. **c**
3. **a**
4. **a**
5. **c**
6. **a**
7. **c**
8. **True.** The Rinspeed Splash is a car that turns into a boat with the push of a button.
9. **True.** The Levitating Hover Scooter speeds above the ground at up to 15 miles an hour (24 kph).
10. **b**
11. **d**
12. **d**

Game Show: Ultimate Science Challenge pages 152-153

1. **a**
2. **b**
3. **True.** The largest bacterium, *Thiomargarita namibiensis*, is up to .75 millimeters (750 micrometers) wide.
4. **c**
5. **b**
6. **d**
7. **True.** The world's largest snowflake was 15 inches (38 cm) wide
8. **b**
9. **c**
10. **b**
11. **d**
12. **c**
13. **False.** A peanut is a type of legume, as are beans and peas.
14. **b**

SCORING

0-44

ON THE LAUNCHPAD

Your interest in science hasn't quite gotten off the ground. But remember that it's all around you, in the sun and the moon, the weather, and the rocks under your feet. Think about how science relates to you, and your interest might just start

45-88

BLASTING OFF

You've learned a lot about how science affects your everyday life and the environment. You like the thrill of learning new things, and that's the first step to making great discoveries. So fasten your seat belt, because you're ready for liftoff!

89-133

SHOOTING FOR THE MOON

The sky is the limit to your science savvy. Your room is probably packed with science fair projects and cool gadgets. Keep tinkering, and you might follow in the footsteps of inventors such as Thomas Edison and Steve Jobs! Just be sure to ask your parents before you decide to take apart the TV set.

Amazing ADVENTURES

WANT TO MAKE A BET? TAILS I LAND FIRST.

SKYDIVERS

Extreme SPORTS

True or false? It's possible to surf down volcanoes.

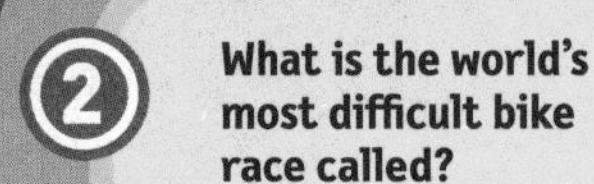

What is the world's most difficult bike race called?

a. Tour de France
b. Boston Marathon
c. Kentucky Derby
d. Yukon Quest

What are BASE jumpers?

a. baseball players who often hit doubles and triples
b. people who jump out of airplanes at military bases
c. climbers who visit base camps on the way up a mountain
d. daredevils who use parachutes to dive from tall structures

During the Empire State Building Run-Up, racers run up how many steps to reach the top of this famous skyscraper in New York, New York, U.S.A.?

a. 356
b. 945
c. 1,576
d. 3,500

True or false? Cliff diving was once considered a test of courage and loyalty to a Hawaiian king.

What is the name of the dizzying sport in which you roll down a hill inside a giant ball?

a. Zorbing
b. ballooning
c. bouncing
d. hamster wheeling

7 **Snowboarders perform extreme jumps, twists, and flips in a U-shaped ramp called what?**

a. a skeleton track
b. a half-pipe
c. an ice rink
d. a stovepipe

8 **How is street luge different from the luge event in the Olympic games?**

a. riders lie down on their sleds
b. riders don't use sleds
c. riders wear helmets
d. street luge takes place on a paved road

9 **What extreme sport involves jumping off a bridge while connected to a long elastic cord?**

a. jumping rope
b. skydiving
c. bungee jumping
d. elastic gymnastics

10 **What is the name of the famous sled-dog race in which dogs race 1,150 miles (1,851 km) from Anchorage to Nome, Alaska, U.S.A.?**

a. Ruff Race
b. Polar Express
c. Iditarod
d. Alaska Purchase

11 **In some motocross events, athletes perform flips in the air while riding on what?**

a. a helicopter
b. a skateboard
c. a motorcycle
d. a goat

12 **Which ancient people invented the sport of surfing?**

a. Vikings
b. Aztec
c. Romans
d. Polynesians

CHECK YOUR ANSWERS ON PAGES 172-173.

THE WILD WEST

1 Which of the following is *not* one of the things cowboys used their **hats** for?

a. to fan fires
b. to keep out the sun
c. to hold water for drinking
d. to cook food in

2 **True or false?** Some of the first cowboys in the American West were from Mexico.

3 In the late 1800s, more than 300,000 people headed to this state to **find gold.**

a. Pennsylvania
b. Wyoming
c. California
d. Florida

4 Why did cowboys wear **spurs** on their boots?

a. to stitch saddles
b. to balance when they walked
c. to prod their horses to go faster
d. to look cool

5 From 1860 to 1861 horseback riders carried **mail across the U.S.** from East to West. What was this service called?

a. the Pony Express
b. the U.S. Postal Service
c. the Rough Rider Express
d. Maverick Mail

6 **Buffalo hunter** William Frederick Cody became a famous showman of the Wild West. What was his nickname?

a. Wild Bill Hickok
b. Buffalo Bill
c. Billy the Kid
d. Pawnee Bill Lillie

7 After a long day of herding cattle, cowboys returned to camp and **chowed down** on what kind of food?

a. spaghetti
b. biscuits and beans
c. hamburgers
d. cupcakes

8 What cowgirl and entertainer earned the nickname "Little Sure Shot" for her sharp-shooting skills?

a. Calamity Jane
b. Annie Oakley
c. Connie Reeves
d. Lucille Mulhall

9 Which of the following people was *not* a Native American chief?

a. Sitting Bull
b. Crazy Horse
c. Looking Glass
d. Sacagawea

10 Who were the "forty-niners" of the American West?

a. people who searched for gold in 1849
b. a football team
c. people who lived in Alaska, the 49th state to join the union
d. 49-year-olds

11 Butch Cassidy was a member of a gang of train robbers. Who was his famous sidekick?

a. Jesse James
b. The Sundance Kid
c. Billy the Kid
d. The Lone Ranger

12 If you were a cowboy in the Wild West, which of the following dangers would you have faced?

a. cattle stampedes
b. Indian attacks
c. bad weather
d. all of the above

13 True or false? American pioneer Daniel Boone wore a coonskin cap.

14 Which breed of horse roamed freely across the West?

a. mustangs
b. Clydesdales
c. Arabians
d. Shetland ponies

15 What were the wagons called that delivered food and cooking equipment to cowboys?

a. chuck wagons
b. stagecoaches
c. chariots
d. minivans

ON SAFARI

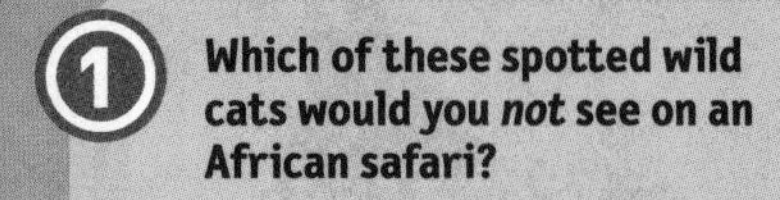

1 **Which of these spotted wild cats would you *not* see on an African safari?**

a. leopard
b. cheetah
c. serval
d. jaguar

2 **True or false?** Giraffes sleep standing up.

3 **African elephants use their trunks to do all of the following except ____.**

a. drink water
b. smell
c. breathe while swimming
d. hold on to baby elephants to keep them close by

GIRAFFE

Ostriches cannot do which of the following?

a. fly
b. run
c. kick
d. lay eggs

OSTRICHES

True or false? All male lions have manes.

Which of these animals migrate in groups of more than a million?

a. wild dogs
b. ostriches
c. wildebeests
d. black mamba snakes

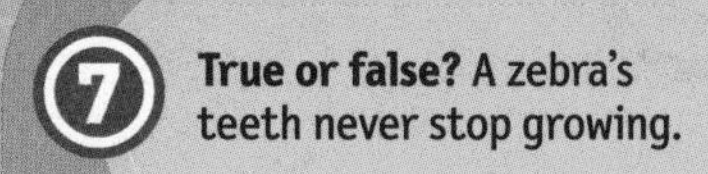

7 **True or false?** A zebra's teeth never stop growing.

8 **Why do Nile crocodiles bask in the sun?**

a. to warm up their bodies
b. it makes them look harmless to their prey
c. to catch their breath after a swim
d. to get a suntan

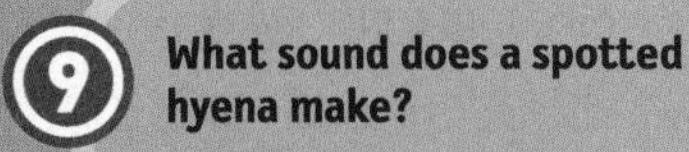

9 **What sound does a spotted hyena make?**

a. meowing
b. roaring
c. whistling
d. laughing

10 **Hippos are water-loving mammals that are closely related to which animals?**

a. whales
b. polar bears
c. rhinos
d. house cats

MOUNTAIN ZEBRA

11 **Which of the following apes would you find in Africa?**

a. orangutans
b. chimpanzees
c. gorillas
d. both b and c

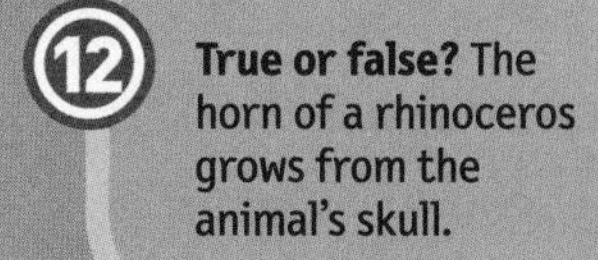

12 **True or false?** The horn of a rhinoceros grows from the animal's skull.

AFRICAN WESTERN LOWLAND GORILLA

CHECK YOUR ANSWERS ON PAGES 172-173.

TRUE or FALSE?

Survival Tips

1. SOS STANDS FOR "SAVE OUR SOULS."
2. IT'S IMPOSSIBLE FOR A PERSON TO DROWN IN QUICKSAND.
3. IF YOU GET FROSTBITE, YOU SHOULD RUB YOUR HANDS TOGETHER TO KEEP THEM WARM.
4. IF YOU'RE IN A CAR WHEN A HURRICANE HITS, IT'S SAFEST TO MOVE THE CAR TO LOW GROUND.
5. IF YOU COME FACE-TO-FACE WITH A COUGAR, YOU SHOULD RUN AWAY AS FAST AS YOU CAN.
6. CLOTHES WITH FLOWERY PATTERNS CAN ATTRACT INSECTS IN THE RAIN FOREST.
7. TO AVOID SLIPPING IT'S BETTER TO ZIGZAG DOWN AN ICY MOUNTAIN SLOPE RATHER THAN SKI IN A STRAIGHT LINE.
8. YOU CAN POUR SALT WATER ON A LEECH TO REMOVE IT FROM YOUR BODY.
9. IF YOU GET CAUGHT IN A ROCKFALL, YOU SHOULD MAKE LIKE A PANCAKE AND LIE FLAT ON THE GROUND.
10. IT'S A BAD IDEA TO KEEP FOOD INSIDE A TENT WHEN YOU'RE CAMPING IN THE WILD.
11. TO STOP SEEING MIRAGES IN THE DESERT—SUCH AS POOLS OF WATER THAT AREN'T ACTUALLY THERE—YOU SHOULD CLIMB TO THE TOP OF A SAND DUNE.
12. IT'S A GOOD IDEA TO BE AS LOUD AS POSSIBLE WHEN YOU'RE HIKING THROUGH BEAR COUNTRY.
13. IF YOU'RE TREKKING ACROSS A GLACIER, IT'S DANGEROUS TO ROPE YOURSELF TO OTHER MEMBERS OF YOUR GROUP IN CASE THEY FALL INTO A CREVASSE.
14. YOU SHOULD STAY AWAY FROM TREES IF YOU GET CAUGHT OUTSIDE DURING A LIGHTNING STORM.
15. YOU ARE MORE LIKELY TO BECOME SHARK FOOD IF YOU WEAR A YELLOW SWIMSUIT IN SHARK-INFESTED WATERS.

16 YOUR BEST CHANCE OF ESCAPE FROM AN ALLIGATOR'S JAWS IS TO PUNCH IT IN THE NOSE.

17 STANDING IN A DOOR FRAME WILL PROTECT YOU DURING AN EARTHQUAKE.

18 IF YOU'RE ON A BOAT DURING A TSUNAMI WARNING, YOU'LL BE SAFER IF YOU SPEED TOWARD DEEPER WATER.

19 IF YOU GET SUCKED UP BY A TORNADO, YOU HAVE A BETTER CHANCE OF SURVIVING IF YOU ARE INSIDE A CAR.

20 THE EMERGENCY WORD "MAYDAY" COMES FROM A DISASTER THAT HAPPENED DURING THE MONTH OF MAY.

21 YOU CAN OUTRUN LAVA DURING A VOLCANIC ERUPTION.

22 IF YOU'RE CAMPING IN THE DESERT, YOU SHOULD KEEP YOUR BOOTS INSIDE YOUR TENT TO PREVENT SCORPIONS FROM CRAWLING INSIDE THEM.

23 IF YOU'RE RIDING A RUNAWAY CAMEL, IT'S BEST TO STAY LOW AND PULL THE REINS TIGHT TO PUT AN END TO YOUR *BUMPY* RIDE.

24 IF YOU SEE A SNAKE, YOU SHOULD JUMP UP AND DOWN AND SHOUT TO SCARE IT AWAY.

25 IF YOU'RE STRANDED OUTSIDE IN A BLIZZARD AND CAN'T FIND SHELTER, IT'S SAFEST TO RUN LIKE THE HOWLING WIND UNTIL YOU FIND HELP.

26 THE BEST WAY TO ESCAPE A CHARGING RHINOCEROS IS TO JUMP INTO ANY THORNY BUSH YOU CAN FIND.

27 TO ESCAPE A HERD OF STAMPEDING ELEPHANTS YOU SHOULD RUN DOWN A HILL AS FAST AS YOU CAN.

28 YOU SHOULD NOT WAVE YOUR ARMS IF YOUR CLOTHING CATCHES FIRE.

29 IF YOU ACCIDENTALLY DISTURB A KILLER-BEE HIVE, YOU SHOULD TAKE A PLUNGE INTO THE FIRST BODY OF WATER YOU CAN FIND.

30 IF YOU'RE CAUGHT IN AN AVALANCHE, CUPPING YOUR HAND OVER YOUR MOUTH WILL HELP YOU SURVIVE.

CHECK YOUR ANSWERS ON PAGES 172-173.

AMUSEMENT PARK THRILLS

1 Which of the following words appears in the most amusement park names?

a. great
b. fun
c. super
d. adventure

2 What's the longest amount of time spent on a Ferris wheel?

a. 1 hour, 15 minutes
b. 6 hours
c. 30 hours, 35 seconds
d. 72 hours

3 Which of these amusement park rides was invented first?

a. merry-go-round
b. Tilt-a-Whirl
c. bumper cars
d. Ferris wheel

4 Where would you find the world's fastest roller coaster, called the Formula Rossa?

a. Ocean Park, in Hong Kong
b. Walt Disney World, in Florida, U.S.A.
c. Abu Dhabi Ferrari World, in the United Arab Emirates
d. Six Flags Mexico, in Mexico City

5 True or false? The first amusement parks were called pleasure gardens.

6 The Colossus roller coaster in England's Thorpe Park has more vertical loops than any other roller coaster in the world. How many does it have?

a. 3
b. 7
c. 10
d. 25

7 What is is the **most popular** amusement park food in the United States?

a. funnel cake
b. cotton candy
c. hot dogs
d. ice cream

8 Lego models of which of these sights are on display in **Legoland** parks around the world?

a. Stonehenge
b. the White House
c. the Eiffel Tower
d. all of the above

9 What is the Guinness **World Record** for the most amusement park visits by one person?

a. 50 visits
b. 585 visits
c. 900 visits
d. 1,108 visits

10 **True or false?** Some experts believe that the first roller coaster was built for Catherine the Great of Russia in 1784.

11 There are **Disney** theme parks in which of the following cities?

a. Tokyo, Japan
b. Paris, France
c. Hong Kong
d. all of the above

12 The "barrel of fun," funny mirrors, and ball pits are **found in ___.**

a. an amusement park bathroom
b. a Tilt-a-Whirl ride
c. a fun house
d. a bumper-car ride

13 What do you call the **Ferris wheel** cars that you sit in as you go around?

a. gondolas
b. baskets
c. boats
d. trains

14 You need a **mallet** to play which popular amusement park game?

a. Ball and Basket
b. Whac-a-Mole
c. Duck Pond
d. Skee-Ball

CHECK YOUR ANSWERS ON PAGES 172-173.

MAP MANIA!

FAMOUS FIRSTS

Find out how much you know about some of the world's most famous adventurers and explorers. Then try to match each feat to the correct location on the map.

NORTH AMERICA

A

B

C

SOUTH AMERICA

1 NORTH POLE

Who were the first people to reach this icy region, in 1909?

a. Neil Armstrong and Buzz Aldrin
b. Meriwether Lewis and William Clark
c. Robert Peary and Matthew Henson
d. Antony and Cleopatra

FIRST EXPEDITION TO REACH THE NORTH POLE

2 SOUTH POLE

Which Norwegian explorer was the first to reach the bottom of the world in 1911?

a. Roald Amundsen
b. Marco Polo
c. Christopher Columbus
d. Amerigo Vespucci

ANTARCTICA

3 KITTY HAWK

In 1903 Orville and Wilbur Wright flew the first powered aircraft off of a beach in the United States. What was the name of the aircraft?

a. *The Wright Flyer*
b. *The Hawk*
c. *The Flying Kitty*
d. *The Concorde*

REPLICA OF THE WRIGHT BROTHERS PLANE

4 MOUNT EVEREST

In 1953 Sir Edmund Hillary and Tenzing Norgay became the first two people to summit the world's tallest mountain. After two months of climbing, how long did they stay at the top?

a. fifteen minutes
b. one hour
c. three hours
d. overnight

EUROPE
ASIA
F
AFRICA
AUSTRALIA
ANTARCTICA

5 AMAZON RIVER

British Army captain Ed Stafford was the first person to walk the length of this wild river. How long did it take him?

a. one hour
b. two weeks
c. a little more than two years
d. almost ten years

6 FLORIDA

Juan Ponce de Léon was the first European explorer to set foot in Florida, in 1513, and gave the place its name. What was the explorer looking for?

a. SeaWorld
b. the Great Pyramid
c. the Fountain of Youth
d. orange trees

MATCH EACH OF THESE HISTORIC FIRSTS TO THE RED MARKER THAT SHOWS WHERE IT TOOK PLACE.

CHECK YOUR ANSWERS ON PAGES 172-173.

GAME SHOW ULTIMATE ADVENTURE CHALLENGE

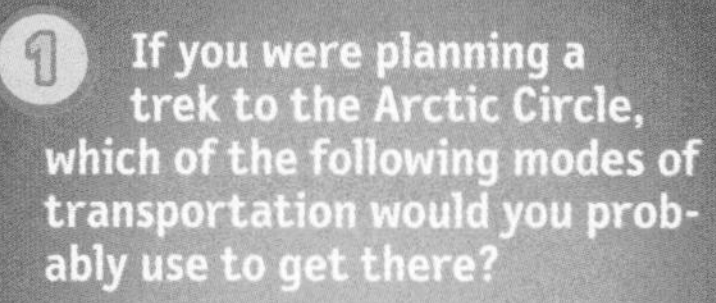

1. If you were planning a trek to the Arctic Circle, which of the following modes of transportation would you probably use to get there?
   a. dogsled
   b. snowmobile
   c. airplane
   d. all of the above

2. The first successful nonstop _______ trip around the world took place in 1999.

a. Jet Ski

b. hot-air balloon

c. helicopter

d. Wienermobile

3. **TRUE OR FALSE?** Asia's K2 mountain is considered one of the world's most dangerous to climb.

4. Who was the first person to walk on the moon?
   a. John Glenn
   b. Alan Shepard
   c. Yuri Gagarin
   d. Neil Armstrong

5. What was the name of the real-life daredevil who tried to jump over everything on a motorcycle, including Greyhound buses and a shark tank?
   a. Motor Man
   b. Evel Knievel
   c. Charlie Chaplin
   d. Lightning McQueen

6. On which TV reality show do contestants race around the world?
   a. *Survivor*
   b. *The Amazing Race*
   c. *Fear Factor*
   d. *Big Brother*

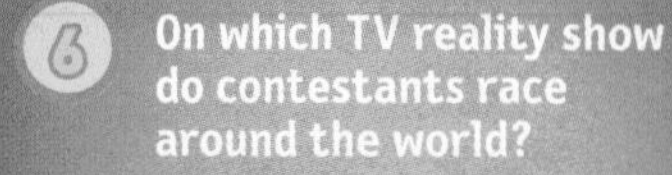

7. Which famous book describes the adventures of a family that is shipwrecked on an island?
   a. *Treasure Island*
   b. *The Swiss Family Robinson*
   c. *Stormbreaker*
   d. *Lemony Snicket's A Series of Unfortunate Events*

8 During the Tour de France, cyclists travel a grueling 2,200 miles (3,600 km) in about three weeks. Which athlete has come in first seven times, the world record for the most wins?

a. Cadel Lee Evans
b. Greg LeMond
c. Lance Armstrong
d. Alberto Contador

9 Which famous person fought at the 1836 Battle of the Alamo in Texas (then part of Mexico)?

a. Davy Crockett
b. Vasco de Gama
c. Abraham Lincoln
d. Leif Ericson

10 Which of the following adventure movies is not part of the *Indiana Jones* series?

a. *Raiders of the Lost Ark*
b. *Temple of Doom*
c. *Kingdom of the Crystal Skull*
d. *On Stranger Tides*

11 Although Christopher Columbus traveled to the Americas with three ships, he returned with two. Which ship was wrecked on the return trip?

a. *Niña*
b. *Pinta*
c. *Santa María*
d. *Titanic*

12 If you were in a sled-dog race, which of the following dog breeds would get you to the finish line the fastest?

a. Pomeranian
b. Dalmatian
c. husky
d. English bulldog

13 What is the name of the U.S. Navy's flight squadron that performs stunts at air shows?

a. The Winged Wonders
b. The Blue Angels
c. The Birds
d. The Daredevils

14 In 1985, Richard Bass became the first person to scale the Seven Summits, the highest mountain on each of the seven continents. Which of the following is *not* one of the Seven Summits?

a. Mount Everest in Asia
b. Vinson Massif in Antarctica
c. Mount Kilimanjaro in Africa
d. Mount St. Helens in North America

15 ULTIMATE BRAIN BUSTER

What is the extreme sport shown in this picture called?

a. wakeboarding
b. skyboarding
c. heli-skiing
d. parasailing

CHECK YOUR ANSWERS ON PAGES 172-173.

ANSWERS

Extreme Sports, pages 158-159

1. **True.** Volcano surfers hike to the top of volcanoes, strap on plywood boards, then ride down the ash slope.
2. **a**
3. **d**
4. **c**
5. **True**. Cliff diving began in 1770, when Hawaiian King Kahekili jumped off a cliff and into the Pacific Ocean. Soon he required his warriors to prove their loyalty by performing the same dive.
6. **a**
7. **b**
8. **d**
9. **c**
10. **c**
11. **c**
12. **d**

The Wild West, pages 160-161

1. **d**
2. **True.** Mexican *vaqueros* drove cattle from New Mexico to Mexico City. In fact, the word cowboy comes from the Spanish word, *vaquero,* which means cowmen.
3. **c**
4. **c**
5. **a**
6. **b**
7. **b**
8. **b**
9. **d**
10. **a**
11. **b**
12. **d**
13. **False.** Daniel Boone preferred to wear felt hats. The image of Boone in a coonskin cap likely comes from the *Daniel Boone* TV show in the 1960s.
14. **a**
15. **a**

On Safari, pages 162-163

1. **d**
2. **False.** Giraffes lie down to sleep. They sleep up to 30 minutes each day.
3. **d**
4. **a**
5. **False.** In East Africa, some male lions do not have manes.
6. **c**
7. **True.** Although a zebra's teeth grow throughout its entire life, grazing and chewing wears them down.
8. **a**
9. **d**
10. **a**
11. **d**
12. **False.** A rhinoceros's horn grows from its skin.

True or False? Survival Tips, pages 164-165

1. **False.** SOS does not stand for anything. It was first used by the German government in 1905 before becoming the worldwide signal for distress.
2. **True.** The human body is less dense than sand, so the deepest you'll sink is to your waist.
3. **False.** Rubbing can cause more damage. The best thing to do is to immediately seek medical aid.
4. **False.** Lower areas are more prone to flooding during a hurricane, so it's better to move the car to high ground.
5. **False.** If you run, the cougar will likely chase you like it does prey. Stay put and makes yourself look as big as possible by raising your arms and spreading out your jacket.
6. **True.** Insects may mistake flowery clothing for actual flowers—and that will put you at risk of being bitten or stung.
7. **True.** Skiing in a zigzag fashion instead of heading straight down the mountain will decrease your chances of slipping.
8. **False.** Move one of your fingernails under the thin part of the leech, then use another fingernail to pry the slimy bugger off your body.
9. **False.** Roll into a ball to protect your head and neck.
10. **True.** Food attracts animals, so stuff your snacks inside a bag and hang them from a tree.
11. **True.** The bending of light rays in the desert heat causes mirages. You are more likely to see mirages closer to the desert floor where the air is the hottest. Moving to higher ground where the air is cooler may make these visions go away.
12. **True.** Bears usually attack when they feel surprised or threatened. Making noise warns the bear of your presence.
13. **False.** If you fall into a crack in the ice, called a crevasse, being tied to your buddies may help stop your fall. Then the group can use the rope to pull you out.
14. **True.** Lightning usually strikes the tallest thing in its path, often trees.
15. **True.** Shark researchers jokingly call the color "yum yum yellow." Sharks are likely attracted to the color because it's easy to spot in the water.
16. **True.** Alligators often open their mouths when tapped or punched on the snout.
17. **False.** Door frames are no stronger than any other part of a house. A better move is to duck under a strong desk or table.
18. **True.** In deep water, you may not even notice a tsunami wave passing under your boat. But tsunamis become especially deadly when the massive waves reach shore.
19. **False.** Chances of surviving being sucked up by a tornado are low, even if you are in a car. Your best bet is to hightail it away from the car and jump in a ditch; it will help shelter you from flying debris.

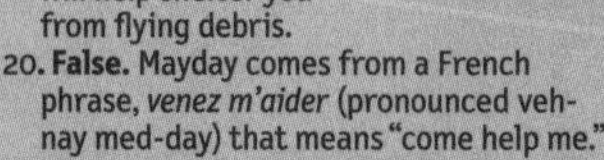

20. **False.** Mayday comes from a French phrase, *venez m'aider* (pronounced veh-nay med-day) that means "come help me."
21. **True.** Lava often moves slowly down the slope of a volcano.
22. **False.** Place boots upside down on top of sticks that you've laid across the ground. Shake your boots out before putting them on.
23. **True.** Pulling on the reins will make the camel run in circles. Eventually, the animal will get tired and stop. Until then, hang on!
24. **False.** Snakes attack when they feel threatened, so back away slowly.
25. **False.** A blizzard's strong, icy winds can be deadly. Dig a snow cave for protection.
26. **True.** Rhinos get prickly around thorns.
27. **True.** The elephants will be less likely to chase you down a hill.
28. **True.** Waving your arms will fan the flames. Instead, stop, drop to the ground, and roll to smother the flames.
29. **False.** The bees will be waiting for you when you come out. Instead, run as far away as you can.
30. **True.** You can create an air pocket with your hand if you're buried alive.

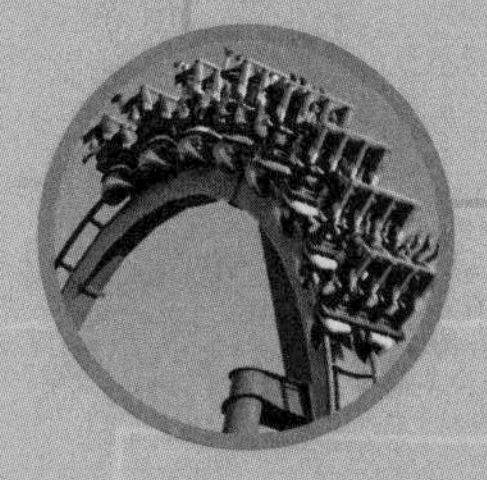

Amusement Park Thrills, pages 166-167

1. **b**
2. **c**
3. **a**
4. **c**
5. **True.** Pleasure gardens, which began in Europe in 1550, featured rides, games, music, and flower gardens.
6. **c**
7. **a**
8. **d**
9. **d**
10. **True.** The ride consisted of wheeled carts that did not lock to the track.
11. **d**
12. **c**
13. **a**
14. **b**

Map Mania! Famous Firsts, pages 168-169

1. **c**
2. **a**
3. **a**
4. **a**
5. **c**
6. **c**
7. **North Pole - D**
8. **South Pole - E**
9. **Kitty Hawk - A**
10. **Mount Everest - F**
11. **Amazon River - C**
12. **Florida - B**

Game Show: Ultimate Adventure Challenge, pages 170-171

1. **d**
2. **b**
3. **True.** Fewer people have made it to the top of K2 than have reached the summit of Mount Everest. K2 is the second tallest mountain in the world after Everest, but frequent storms can make it more difficult to climb.
4. **d**
5. **b**
6. **b**
7. **b**
8. **c**
9. **a**
10. **d**
11. **c**
12. **c**
13. **b**
14. **d**
15. **b**

SCORING

0-37

COME OUT OF YOUR SHELL

It's cool to watch people trek into the Amazon on TV, but you prefer to keep your feet planted firmly in your own zip code. But where would we be if people had never left their caves and explored the world beyond? Take it one step at a time and find your inner explorer.

38-74

SURVIVOR

You've got a taste for exploration and a lot of common sense to keep you safe. That's a great combination! If you get into a bit of a rut once in a while, find a new adventure and you'll be back in action in no time.

75-110

THRILL SEEKER!

For you, it's "Go big or go home!" You have tons of energy and are a bit of a daredevil. Hiking, skateboarding, mountain climbing, you love it all! Just remember to stay safe when you go out there and conquer the world.

Cover
(aircraft), Barbara Ries; (dog), Mark Gsellman/Getty Images; (frog), Alptraum/Dreamstime; (money), ©Stock Connection/SuperStock; (ice cream), Olga Lyubkina/Shutterstock; (king tut), KENNETH GARRETT/National Geographic Stock; (Background), David Arts/Shutterstock

Back Cover
(lightning), Alhovik/Dreamstime; (Kitten), Anna Utekhina/Dreamstime

Spine
(Dog) Mark Gsellman/Getty Images

Front Matter
1 (LO), KENNETH GARRETT/National Geographic Stock; 1 (UP), Mark Gsellman/Getty Images; 2-3 (Background), David Arts/Shutterstock; 4 (UP LE), Edwin Verin/Dreamstime; 4 (LO LE), oversnap/iStockphoto; 4 (UP RT), ©Paramount/courtesy Everett Collection; 4 (LO RT), DROR MADAR/National Geographic My Shot; 5 (UP LE), Gail Johnson/Dreamstime; 5 (LO RT), Germanskydiver/Shutterstock; 5 (LO LE), Padede/Dreamstime; 5 (LO RT), charles taylor/Shutterstock; 6, charles taylor/Shutterstock; 7, Angelika/iStockphoto.

Animal Intelligence (8-33)
8-9 (Background), Edwin Verin/Dreamstime; 8 (UP), Todd Taulman/Dreamstime; 9 (Ctr), Olga Lyubkina/Shutterstock; 10 (Up), Tomas Sereda/Dreamstime; 10 (LO), Joseph Moran/Dreamstime; 11 (UP), Mike Hill/Getty Images; 11 (LO LE), jwebb/iStockphoto; 12-13, Franco Tempesta; 14-15, Jagronick/Dreamstime; 16 (LE), Elena Butinova/Shutterstock; 16 (UP RT), bobbieo/iStockphoto; 16 (LO RT), jodymenard/iStockphoto; 17 (LE), Alistair Scott/Dreamstime; 17 (RT), Isselee/Dreamstime; 20 (UP LE), Adogslifephoto/Dreamstime; 20 (UP RT), Giuseppe Lancia/Dreamstime; 20 (LO RT), Nikolay Okhitin/Dreamstime; 21 (LO), Isselee/Dreamstime; 22 (1), B & T Media Group Inc./Shutterstock; 22 (2), THOMAS MARENT/ MINDEN PICTURES/National Geographic Stock; 22 (3), Achim Baque/Shutterstock; 22 (4), Cuson/Shutterstock; 22 (5), Stormcastle/Dreamstime; 22 (6), Angel Sosa/Dreamstime; 23 (7), GERRY ELLIS/ DIGITAL VISIONS; 23 (8), TOM MCHUGH/Getty Images; 23 (9), Andy Rouse/Getty Images; 23 (10), Jan Pokorný/Dreamstime; 23 (11), Steve Allen/Dreamstime; 23 (12), Anan Kaewkhammul/Shutterstock; 24-25, Ch'ien Lee/Minden Pictures; 26-27 (12), António Jorge Da Silva Nunes/Dreamstime; 28 (UP LE), smellme/Dreamstime; 28 (UP RT), Alle/Dreamstime; 28 (LO LE), Alexander Spegalskiy/Dreamstime; 28 (LO RT), tubeceo/Shutterstock; 29 (UP), mlorenz/shutterstock; 29 (LO), YVA MOMATIUK & JOHN EASTCOTT/MINDEN PICTURES/National Geographic Stock; 30-31 (Background), Davidarts/Dreamstime; 30 (UP LE), Dan Sipple; 30 (CTR), DAVID DOUBILET/National Geographic Stock; 30 (LO LE), Aetmeister/Dreamstime; 30 (LO RT), Lukas Gojda/Dreamstime; 31 (UP LE), Digital Vision/PictureQuest; 31 (UP RT-A), Nikolai Tsvetkov/Dreamstime; 31 (UP RT-B), Anna Bakulina/Dreamstime; 31 (UP RT-C), Liliya Kulianionak/Shutterstock; 31 (UP RT-D), Karen Givens/Shutterstock; 31 (CTR), Neal Cooper/Dreamstime; 31 (LO), belizar/Shutterstock; 32 (LE), Joseph Moran/Dreamstime; 33 (UP LE), Ch'ien Lee/Minden Pictures; 33 (UP RT), Karen Givens/Shutterstock; 33 (LO LE), DNY59/istockphoto; 33 (LO CTR), Snowleopard1/istockphoto; 33 (LO RT), LordRunar/istockphoto

Around the World (34-55)
34-35, oversnap/iStockphoto; 36 (UP LE), Vakhrushev Pavel/Shutterstock; 36-37 (LO), kamisoka/iStockphoto; 38-39, Jabiru/Dreamstime; 40 (UP), Jun Yan Loke/Dreamstime; 40 (CTR), Linqong/Dreamstime; 40 (LO LE), Andrey Armyagov/Shutterstock; 40 (LO RT), Tatiana Popova/Shutterstock; 41 (LE), Archinte/Dreamstime; 41 (RT), Monkey Business Images/Shutterstock; 42 (UP), Vulnificans/Dreamstime; 42 (CTR), Lobacheveb/Dreamstime; 42 (LO-A), Erik Mandre/Dreamstime; 42 (LO-B), Dave_cgn/Dreamstime; 42 (LO-C), Richard Hermann/Visuals Unlimited, Inc./Getty Images; 42 (LO-D), Joop Snijder jr./Shutterstock; 43 (UP), AHMAD FAIZAL YAHYA/Shutterstock; 43 (LO), ManoAfrica/iStockphoto; 46 (UP), Emjaysea/Dreamstime; 46 (LO LE), Smit/Shutterstock; 46 (RT), Pichugin Dmitry/Shutterstock; 47 (UP), Martin Maun/Shutterstock; 47 (CTR), EpicStockMedia/Shutterstock; 47 (LO), gary yim/Shutterstock; 48-49, Speedfighter17/Dreamstime; 50 (UP), Rudolf Tepfenhart/Shutterstock; 50 (CTR), Celso Diniz/Dreamstime; 50 (LO LE), Samot/Shutterstock; 50 (LO RT), holbox/Shutterstock; 51 (UP), itsskin/iStockphoto; 51 (LO LE), LUIS MARDEN/National Geographic Stock; 51 (LO RT), TANAWAT LIKITKERERAT/National Geographic My Shot/National Geographic Stock; 52-53 (Background), Davidarts/Dreamstime; 52 (UP LE), Dan Sipple; 52 (RT), travellinglight/iStockphoto; 53 (UP), Massimiliano Ferrarini/Dreamstime; 53 (CTR-a), Skutvik/Dreamstime; 53 (CTR-b), Geopappas/Dreamstime; 53 (CTR-c), Richard Gunion/Dreamstime; 53 (CTR-d), Pierdelune/Dreamstime; 53 (LO-A), Fedor Sidorov/Dreamstime; 53 (LO-b), Vacclav/Shutterstock; 53 (LO-c), Dan Breckwoldt/Dreamstime; 53 (LO-d), Nico Smit/Dreamstime; 54 (UP LE), Stuart Corlett/Dreamstime; 54 (UP RT), Jamie Roach/Shutterstock; 54 (LO), Monkey Business Images/Shutterstock; 55 (UP LE), Cheryl Casey/Dreamstime; 55 (UP RT), Fedor Sidorov/Dreamstime; 55 (LO LE), Diego Vito Cervo/Dreamstime; 55 (LO CTR), Bc-photo/Dreamstime; 55 (LO RT), JetKat/Shutterstock

Pop Culture (56-71)
56-57, ©Paramount/courtesy Everett Collection; 58 (UP), mgkaya/iStockphoto;
58 (LO), AP Images/PRNewsFoto/Nickelodeon/Lisa Rose; 59 (UP), ©MCMXCII CBS INC. All Rights Reserved / Everett Collection, Inc.; 59 (LO), Everett Collection Inc/Alamy; 60, © Marvel Comics; 64 (UP), sonny2962/iStockphoto; 64 (LO LE), Aaron Settipane/Dreamstime; 64 (LO RT), Denis Makarenko/Dreamstime; 65 (UP), Featureflash/Shutterstock; 65 (LO), SteveChristensen/iStockphoto; 66-67 (Background), Athanasia Nomikou/Shutterstock; 68-69 (Background), Davidarts/Dreamstime; 68 (UP LE), Dan Sipple; 68 (UP RT), Everett Collection, Inc.; 68 (LO), Ron Tom/Disney Channel via Getty Images; 69 (UP LE), Joe Seer/Shutterstock; 69 (UP RT-a), Neale Cousland/Shutterstock; 69 (UP RT-b), Ethan Miller/WireImage/Getty Images; 69 (UP RT-C), Sergei Bachlakov/Shutterstock; 69 (UP RT-D), s_bukley/Shutterstock; 69 (Lo-a), ©Buena Vista Pictures/courtesy Everett Collection; 69 (LO-b), ©Buena Vista Pictures/courtesy Everett Collection; 69 (lo-c), ©Buena Vista Pictures/courtesy Everett Collection; 69 (lo-D), ©Buena Vista Pictures/courtesy Everett Collection; 70 (LE), AP Photo/Mary Altaffer; 70 (RT), ©Buena Vista Pictures/courtesy Everett Collection; 71 (UP LE), Denis Makarenko/Dreamstime; 71 (LO LE), beyond/CORBIS; 71 (LO CTR), LeggNet/iStockphoto; 71 (LO RT), Jeffrey Coolidge/Getty Images

The Great Outdoors (72-91)
72, DROR MADAR/National Geographic My Shot; 73, Mark Grenier/Shutterstock; 74 (UP), THEPALMER/iStockphoto; 74 (LE ctr), ElementalImaging/iStockphoto; 74 (RT CTR), the4js/iStockphoto; 74 (LO LE), Sean Murray/Dreamstime; 74 (LO RT), Dmitrijs Bindemanis/Shutterstock; 75 (UP), NTCo/iStockphoto; 75 (LO), OliverChilds/iStockphoto; 76, Andreas G. Karelias/Shutterstock; 77, Ruta Saulyte-Laurinaviciene/Shutterstock; 78 (UP), Sergey Uryadnikov/Dreamstime; 78 (CTR), amskad/Shutterstock; 78 (LO RT), Mayskyphoto/Shutterstock; 79 (LO), Lusoimages/Shutterstock; 80-81 (Background), Nejron Photo/Shutterstock; 80 (LO), Denis Tabler/Shutterstock; 81 (LO), 4FR/Shutterstock; 82-83 (Background), Marcos Casiano/Dreamstime; 83 (UP RT), jollyphoto/iStockphoto; 84 (1), Pgiam/iStockphoto; 84 (2), KJA/iStockphoto; 84 (3), John Glade/Shutterstock; 84 (4), Pichugin Dmitry/Shutterstock; 84 (5), dbencek/iStockphoto; 84 (6), Fotomorgana/Dreamstime;
85 (7), Platslee/Shutterstock; 85 (8), Hanis/iStockphoto; 85 (9), ooyoo/iStockphoto; 85 (10), KarenMassier/iStockphoto; 85 (11), NickolayV/iStockphoto; 85 (12), Pal Teravagimov/Shutterstock; 88-89 (Background), Davidarts/Dreamstime; 88 (UP

LE), Dan Sipple; 88 (UP RT), Dimabl/Dreamstime; 88 (LO LE), TIM LAMAN /National Geographic Stock; 88 (LO RT- A), Daniel Budiman/Dreamstime; 88 (LO RT- B), Steveheap/Dreamstime; 88 (LO RT- C), Studio 37/Dreamstime; 88 (LO RT-D), Pavel Mitrofanov/Dreamstime; 89 (UP LE), Isselee/Dreamstime; 89 (UP RT), Vladimir Blinov/Dreamstime; 89 (LO LE), Goinyk Volodymyr/Dreamstime; 89 (LO RT), DAVE BROSHA/National Geographic Stock; 90 (UP RT), hadynyah/iStockphoto; 90 (LO LE), Kmiragaya/Dreamstime; 90 (LO RT), Marcos Casiano/Dreamstime; 91 (UP), TIM LAMAN /National Geographic Stock; 91 (LO LE), PM Images/Getty Images; 91 (LO CTR), Tsekhmister/Dreamstime; 91 (LO RT), Benjamin Todd Shoemake/Dreamstime

Time Machine (92-115)
92-93, Gail Johnson/Dreamstime; 94 (UP), lucafabbian/iStockphoto; 94 (LO LE), DNY59/iStockphoto; 94 (RT), Kristin Smith/ Shutterstock; 95 (UP), inkit/iStockphoto; 95 (LO), HKPNC/iStockphoto; 96-97 (Background), Fer Gregory/Shutterstock; 98 (UP RT), wynnter/iStockphoto; 98 (LO LE), joecicak/iStockphoto; 99 (UP LE), Chip Somodevilla/Getty Images; 99 (LE CTR), Oleg Golovnev/Shutterstock; 99 (LO), Sarah Dreyer/Dreamstime; 100-101, Ken Marschall; 102 (UP), Dio5050/Dreamstime; 102 (CTR), Elena Elisseeva/Shutterstock; 102 (LO LE), 4kodiak/iStockphoto; 103 (UP), beusbeus/iStockphoto; 103 (RT CTR), Ildi Papp/Shutterstock; 103 (LO LE), jenjen42/iStockphoto; 104-105, marco_tb/Shutterstock; 106 (UP), Apic/Getty Images; 106 (CTR), PictureLake/iStockphoto; 106 (LO), rook76/Shutterstock; 107 (UP LE), Neftali/Shutterstock; 107 (UP RT), Bettmann/CORBIS; 107 (LE ctr), traveler1116/iStockphoto; 107 (LO), ©Warner Brothers/Everett Collection, Inc.; 108-109, Lambros Kazan/Shutterstock; 110 (UP), 77zack/Dreamstime; 110 (LO LE), Matt84/iStockphoto; 110 (LO RT), Philcold/ Dreamstime; 111 (UP), ZargonDesign/iStockphoto; 111 (LO LE), patrimonio designs limited/Shutterstock; 111 (LO RT), ULTRA_GENERIC/iStockphoto; 112-113 (Background), Davidarts/Dreamstime; 112 (UP LE), Dan Sipple; 112 (UP RT), Bowie15/ Dreamstime; 112 (LO LE), James Steidl/Shutterstock; 112 (LO RT), margouillat photo/Shutterstock; 113 (UP), Nlizer/ Dreamstime; 113 (UP RT-A), Everett Collection, Inc.; 113 (UP RT-B), John Springer Collection/CORBIS; 113 (UP RT-C), Everett Collection, Inc.; 113 (UP RT-D), Everett Collection, Inc.; 113 (LO RT), JDFiend/iStockphoto; 114 (UP LE), inkit/iStockphoto; 114 (UP RT), joecicak/iStockphoto; 114 (LO), jenjen42/iStockphoto; 115 (UP RT), Nlizer/Dreamstime; 115 (CTR), Matt84/ Shutterstock; 115 (LO LE), knape/iStockphoto; 115 (LO CTR), Joruba/Dreamstime; 115 (LO RT), Serrnovik/Dreamstime

Number Cruncher (116-133)
116-117, Padede/Dreamstime; 118 (UP RT), Michael Ansell/Dreamstime; 118 (UP LE), Natalia Pavlova/Dreamstime; 118 (LO LE), Bruce MacQueen/Shutterstock; 118 (LO RT), Supertrooper/Shutterstock; 119 (UP), Leslie78/Shutterstock; 119 (LO), worldswildlifewonders/Shutterstock; 121, Iain Masterton/Alamy; 122 (LO LE), Ralf Siemieniec/Dreamstime; 126 (UP RT), Feng Yu/Dreamstime; 126 (UP LE), Sergei Bachlakov/Shutterstock; 126 (ctr le), TRINACRIA PHOTO/Shutterstock; 126 (LO RT), Maravic/iStockphoto; 127 (UP LE), Christopher Penler/Shutterstock; 127 (CTR), Jonathan Larsen/Diadem Images/ Alamy; 127 (LO), Olga Besnard/Dreamstime; 128 (UP), Dušan Zidar/Dreamstime; 128 (CTR), marcovarro/Shutterstock; 128 (LO LE), Shebeko/Shutterstock; 129 (UP), Sandra van der Steen/Shutterstock; 129 (CTR), Daniel Loncarevic/Shutterstock; 129 (LO), Timbooth2770/Dreamstime; 130-131 (Background), Davidarts/Dreamstime; 130 (UP LE), Dan Sipple; 130 (UP RT), Mike Flippo/Shutterstock; 130 (LO LE), Creativeye99/iStockphoto; 130 (LO RT), Johnfoto/Dreamstime; 131 (UP), Robin van Lonkhuijsen/Reuters; 131 (CTR le), Givaga/Shutterstock; 131 (CTR rt), bonchan/Shutterstock; 131 (lo-a), Columbia Pictures/ Everett Collection, Inc.; 131 (lo-b), Nickelodeon/Everett Collection, Inc.; 131 (lo-c), ©Universal Pictures/Everett Collection, Inc.; 131 (lo-d), Mary Evans/©:TM & © 2006 DREAMWORKS LLC.© T/Ronald Grant/Everett Collection, Inc.; 132 (UP), Michael Ansell/Dreamstime; 132 (CTR), Ralf Siemieniec/Dreamstime; 132 (LO), Iain Masterton/Alamy; 133 (UP LE), Christopher Penler/Shutterstock; 133 (UP RT), Columbia Pictures/Everett Collection, Inc.; 133 (LO LE), Armandavtyan/Dreamstime; 133 (LO CTR), Cammeraydave/Dreamstime; 133 (LO RT), Barros & Barros/Getty Images

It's Not Rocket Science (134-155)
134-135, charles taylor/Shutterstock; 137, Sebastian Kaulitzki/ Shutterstock; 138, Tyler Olson/Shutterstock; 139, KIM KYUNG-HOON/Reuters/CORBIS; 140 (UP), Snezhok/Dreamstime; 140 (CTR), Eerik/iStockphoto; 140 (LO), EricHood/iStockphoto; 141 (UP RT), Axleight/Dreamstime; 141 (RT CTR), Regien Paassen/Shutterstock; 141 (LO LE), torsten kuenzlen/Dreamstime; 142-143, Stockbyte/Getty Images; 146-147, imagedepotpro/iStockphoto; 148 (UP RT), Andrea Danti/Shutterstock; 148 (LO RT), dasbild/iStockphoto; 149 (UP RT), Weldon Schloneger/Shutterstock; 149 (LO LE), Ismaeltr/Dreamstime; 149 (LO RT), Saturated/iStockphoto; 150 (UP), Maomaotou/Dreamstime; 150 (LO), Michael Stokes/Shutterstock; 151 (UP), jondpatton/ iStockphoto; 151 (LO), Snaprender/iStockphoto; 152-153 (Background), Davidarts/Dreamstime; 152 (UP LE), Dan Sipple; 152 (UP RT), Hannu Viitanen/Dreamstime; 152 (CTR LE), Paul Marcus/Shutterstock; 152 (LO LE), -Mosquito-/iStockphoto; 153 (UP LE), Cathy Keifer/Shutterstock; 153 (UP RT), CARSTEN PETER/SPELEORESEARCH & FILMS/National Geographic Stock; 153 (LO LE), Natika/Dreamstime; 153 (LO RT-A), Marianne De Jong/Dreamstime; 153 (LO RT-B), Nguyen Thai/Dreamstime; 153 (LO RT-C), Viatcheslav/Dreamstime; 153 (LO RT-D), Joao Virissimo/Dreamstime; 154 (UP), torsten kuenzlen/Dreamstime; 154 (LO LE), KIM KYUNG-HOON/Reuters/CORBIS; 154 (LO RT), Snaprender/iStockphoto; 155 (UP), Michael Stokes/ Shutterstock; 155 (LO LE), Cathy Keifer/Dreamstime; 155 (LO CTR), John A Davis/Shutterstock; 155 (LO RT), Lasse Kristensen/Shutterstock

Amazing Adventures (156-173)
156-157, Germanskydiver/Shutterstock; 158 (UP), Paul Mckinnon/Dreamstime; 158 (LO LE), Eyecandy Images/Alamy; 158 (LO RT), ChurchmouseNZ/iStockphoto; 159 (UP), Martinjaud/Dreamstime; 159 (LO), Cultura Limited/SuperStock; 160-161, Rinus Baak/Dreamstime; 162 (UP LE), Regien Paassen/Dreamstime; 162 (CTR), WLDavies/iStockphoto; 162 (LO LE), Angelika/ iStockphoto; 163 (UP RT), Angelika/iStockphoto; 163 (LO), worldswildlifewonders/Shutterstock; 166-167 (Background), Kyrien/Dreamstime; 168 (UP), ROBERT E PEARY/National Geographic Stock; 168 (LO LE), Pascaline Daniel/Dreamstime; 168 (LO RT), jennyt/shutterstock; 169 (UP), Daniel Prudek/Shutterstock; 169 (LO LE), Dragi Stankovic/Dreamstime; 169 (LO RT), alessandroiryna/iStockphoto; 170-171 (Background), Davidarts/Dreamstime; 170 (UP LE), Dan Sipple; 170 (le-a), crokogen/ iStockphoto; 170 (le-B), gary718/Shutterstock; 170 (le-C), Billyckchan/iStockphoto; 170 (le-D), Red/Dreamstime; 170 (RT), e_wire/iStockphoto; 171 (UP), Sally Scott/Dreamstime; 171 (CTR), rypson/iStockphoto; 171 (LO), Joe McBride/Getty Images; 172 (LE), Paul Mckinnon/Dreamstime; 172 (RT), Rob Stegmann/Dreamstime; 173 (UP LE), Grigor Atanasov/Dreamstime; 173 (UP RT), crokogen/iStockphoto; 173 (LO LE), Photographer/Shutterstock; 173 (LO CTR), migin/iStockphoto; 173 (LO RT), Sportstock/iStockphoto

Published by the National Geographic Society
John M. Fahey, Jr., Chairman of the Board and Chief Executive Officer
Timothy T. Kelly, President
Declan Moore, Executive Vice President; President, Publishing and Digital Media
Melina Gerosa Bellows, Executive Vice President; Chief Creative Officer, Books, Kids, and Family

Prepared by the Book Division
Hector Sierra, Senior Vice President and General Manager
Nancy Laties Feresten, Senior Vice President, Editor in Chief, Children's Books
Jonathan Halling, Design Director, Books and Children's Publishing
Jay Sumner, Director of Photography, Children's Publishing
Jennifer Emmett, Editorial Director, Children's Books
Eva Absher-Schantz, Managing Art Director
Carl Mehler, Director of Maps
R. Gary Colbert, Production Director
Jennifer A. Thornton, Director of Managing Editorial

Staff for This Book
Robin Terry, Project Editor
Eva Absher-Schantz, Art Director
Kelley Miller, Senior Illustrations Editor
Simon Renwick, Designer, Em Dash
Kate Olesin, Assistant Editor
Hillary Moloney, Illustrations Assistant
Lauren Jones, Freelance Photo Editor
Nancy Honovich, Writer/Researcher
Michael McNey and Martin S. Walz, Map Research and Production
Grace Hill, Associate Managing Editor
Joan Gossett, Judy Klein, Production Editors
Lewis R. Bassford, Production Manager
Kathryn Robbins, Design Production Assistant
Susan Borke, Legal and Business Affairs
Maura Welch, Eileen McFarland, Editorial Interns

Manufacturing and Quality Management
Christopher A. Liedel, Chief Financial Officer
Phillip L. Schlosser, Senior Vice President
Chris Brown, Vice President
George Bounelis, Vice President, Production Services
Nicole Elliott, Manager
Rachel Faulise, Manager
Robert L. Barr, Manager

The National Geographic Society is one of the world's largest nonprofit scientific and educational organizations. Founded in 1888 to "increase and diffuse geographic knowledge," the Society works to inspire people to care about the planet. National Geographic reflects the world through its magazines, television programs, films, music and radio, books, DVDs, maps, exhibitions, live events, school publishing programs, interactive media and merchandise. *National Geographic* magazine, the Society's official journal, published in English and 33 local-language editions, is read by more than 38 million people each month. The National Geographic Channel reaches 320 million households in 34 languages in 166 countries. National Geographic Digital Media receives more than 15 million visitors a month. National Geographic has funded more than 9,400 scientific research, conservation and exploration projects and supports an education program promoting geography literacy. For more information, visit nationalgeographic.com.

For more information, please call 1-800-NGS LINE (647-5463) or write to the following address:
National Geographic Society
1145 17th Street N.W.
Washington, D.C. 20036-4688 U.S.A.

Visit us online at
nationalgeographic.com/books

For librarians and teachers:
ngchildrensbooks.org

More for kids from National Geographic:
kids.nationalgeographic.com

For information about special discounts for bulk purchases, please contact National Geographic Books Special Sales:
ngspecsales@ngs.org

For rights or permissions inquiries, please contact National Geographic Books Subsidiary Rights: ngbookrights@ngs.org

Paperback ISBN: 978-1-4263-1018-8
Library ISBN: 978-1-4263-1019-5

Printed in U.S.A.
13/WOR/2